MY NORMANDY

MY NORMANDY

A Teenager Lives through World War II

ARMAND IDRAC

EDITED AND TRANSLATED
FROM THE FRENCH
BY
JOANNE SILVER

Beach Lloyd
PUBLISHERS
LLC

Wayne, Pennsylvania

Beach Lloyd Publishers LLC, October 2005

Idrac, Armand, 1928 –

My Normandy: A Teenager Lives through World War II
Excerpted from Memoirs from Normandy: Childhood, War & Life's Adventures by Armand Idrac; both works translated and edited by Joanne S. Silver.

ISBN: 978-0-9743158-1-2
0-9743158-1-8

Printed in the United States of America

Library of Congress Control Number: 2005929958

Cover design by Book Cover Express and Kevin Bugge;
Computer conversion by Michael Bowe;
Layout and formatting by Ronald Silver;
Photographs by Armand Idrac, Yvonne Idrac, Ronald Silver;
Readability Statistics by Dr. Scott Greenwood,
Literacy Department, West Chester University;
Rhoda Kapner, Reading Specialist;
Microsoft Word 2003.

TRANSLATOR / EDITOR'S NOTE

My sincere thanks to the many family members and friends who encouraged, helped and supported the work of this translation. In particular, the readers who furnished valuable feedback are Joanna Shoestock, Ron Silver and Emily Wagner.

As in the case of the original, full edition, I dedicate this translation to my father, Rex Beach Lloyd, a Navy medic among the American Allies who landed at Omaha Beach on D-Day, June 6, 1944, when Armand was fifteen years old.

Joanne Shoestock Silver—June 6, 2005

CONTENTS

ILLUSTRATIONS

FOREWORD

by Emmanuel Le Roy Ladurie, « Universitaire » and writer, honorary professor of the Collège de France, member of the « Institut de France » and Commander in the French Legion of Honor

Armand Idrac and I have a landing in common. You will read his version inside, in Chapter IV of this work. Now, here is mine, from the beginning to the end of this "episode." You might say that, as a result, for the two of us and for many others on that sixth day of June 1944, the landing was to open a new chapter. For two and a half months, this was an incredible, sometimes frightening, sometimes marvelous, game of cops and robbers. The sky was a beautiful blue: the bombs and the high-explosive shells that the British showered on us, first at my parents' home, then in the pocket of Falaise where we had the strange idea to take refuge, were not very dangerous unless—it goes without saying—they did not fall directly overhead.

My brother, my sisters and I had learned very quickly to recognize the whistling of the bomb or the shell striking at a distance far enough away not to be deadly, at least if one had the presence of mind to get down on the ground. My brother, Jacques Le Roy Ladurie, was in the Resistance of Orléans. My mother lived through unforgivable anguishes; she carted food for the people of our village and for refugees, in trucks, at least one of which was machine-gunned by a plane. She had only enough time to throw herself into a ditch.

Once more, the relation with the occupant did not have the Manichaean simplicity[1] that often came with the passage

[1] That is, viewing the world as divided into good and evil.

of time. The Resistance armed by the Norman adults proved difficult—the country was heavily occupied by the German troops. We didn't trust the SS and the members of the Gestapo, but the scattered relationships that we had with other members of the Wehrmacht were not necessarily hostile. One of them compared me kindly to his son; another complained bitterly about the length of the war; a third congratulated us for staying calm under the bombs. Of course, we longed constantly for the Liberation. The army of General Leclerc was already popular among us. But it all remained strangely abstract. Like a dream.

In the last days of the battle of Falaise, we found ourselves at my grandfather's home in Giel (Orne), in the midst of the army of Vlassov.[2] Elsewhere, members of this army committed horrible acts, that was certain; but here it was a case of draftees wanting to surrender as quickly as possible. They did not imagine that a prison in Siberia awaited them. They negotiated their surrender with a local member of the Resistance, who revealed himself for the first time and in a peacemaking manner, on the very day of this surrender. He took charge of the Vlassovians cautiously and in an easy-going way; they couldn't have asked for anything better. He turned them over to the British, which was expected. At the last moment, these soldiers who had come from the Soviet Union and passed into the German camp got up into the British trucks and tossed a large number of objects—not grenades—on our Resistants. The French, forgetting their dignity, threw themselves to the ground, to gather them up. They were packs of cigarettes. Sent from the captives to their keepers, they symbolized an inglorious reconciliation.

A little distance off, on a roadside, a French civilian of recent hero status was hammering on the heel of the cadaver

---

[2] A Russian general. After having fought in the Red army, he was taken prisoner by the Germans, drafted into their army (1942) and then fought against the Russians. Captured in 1945, he was hanged in 1946.

of a German soldier. A wheelbarrow of mercy appeared, led by a courageous man who loaded the remains of the young enemy, taken from his persecutor. That's how the war ended. Shortly thereafter, I noticed the first Allied soldier, a liberator; I wanted to ask him for sugar, a commodity of which we had been deprived. I gathered all that was left of my English lessons, and pronounced a word that resembled sugar phonetically : *çu-gare.* Following which—mortifying but inevitable misunderstanding—the English soldier reached into his pocket and kindly offered me a cigar.

*

* *

The following is a portion of the journal of the landing, a journal kept by my older sister Marie Le Roy Ladurie, who was sixteen at the time. She sets the stage and tells the story of Armand Idrac coming to our home at the beginning of those three fateful months.

June 6, 1944

2 to 8 a.m.
Continuous rolling of cannons in the direction of Bayeux and Cherbourg.
A lot of planes passing over.

Around 5:30 a.m.
Maman and Emmanuel ride bikes to Caen, to look for Eric [ELRL's[3] cousin] and François [younger brother of ELRL], who have stayed at school; they don't use the car, to get through more easily.

During the morning
John Thibault [ELRL's uncle] arrived by motorcycle: there is a landing (we suspected it!)—Cherbourg, Bayeux, Caen, Cabourg, Le Havre—but in his opinion, a simple diversion in Calvados. Big offensive likely in Somme, Anvers.

---

[3] Emmanuel Le Roy Ladurie's

Some German police bring signs about the state of war: forbidden to circulate except on foot, etc.; to Nicole Martin [ELRL's father's secretary], "now there's war on the coast."
Maman returns with the three boys and the little Revinnac boy. Emmanuel's bike is stolen by a young German soldier.
A little more craziness in Caen; lines in front of the bakeries.
My Aunt Dufaure [will be killed, alas, the following night: sad story! Dead with her husband and eight-year-old daughter] refuses to leave Caen.
Continuous rolling of cannons in the direction of Bayeux.

Wednesday, June 7, 1944
No end to the planes passing over.

Around 5 p.m.
Madame Idrac and her two children, Armand and Arlette, arrive from Caen. They left after a horrible night of bombings.
On fire: Arquette Street, Carmes, Saint Jean, Priminime, Beauséjour, the students' dorm, Malherbe School, etc.
A lot of people from Caen take refuge in the quarries of Fleury.

Thursday, June 8, 1944
Our days and the noise of the planes are inseparable; the moments of silence are astonishing.
Visit of Pierre de Lalonde [John Thibault's friend].
Everything is okay at la Motte [home of John Thibault].

Around 12:30 p.m. there falls:

1. A very small torpedo [aerial bomb], in la Garenne [piece of land belonging to JLRL[4]], rebounding there from the pasture, skimming the corner of the laundry; rightfully so, Madame Bopuquerel (employee) is frightened. Not much

[4] Jacques Le Roy Ladurie, the father of Marie, Emmanuel and François.

damage, the ground scraped, apple trees and poplars uprooted, broken up. About sixty glass panes broken.

2. A large torpedo in la Houssaye [same piece of land], where John [the gardener] was working.

3. A large torpedo in the pasture.
Raoul [a local gardener who is seriously ill] definitely [. . .] (?) stays from now on in the flowered sitting room. The cannons come closer.

Friday, June 9, 1944
Not being artillerymen, our inexperienced ears heard the cannons as being so close by that we expected the British at any moment during the night. We listened for the language that the men used, swearing as they passed in trucks in front of the gate. The heavy gunfire moved off in the distance. Continuous machine-gunning on the road.

Saturday, June 10, 1944
Passage of the planes still just as intense.
Visit of John Thibault (allowed to move about). La Motte, totally evacuated; in three hours has been transformed into the "lazaret"[5] *of Adolph Hitler's division. A half hour after their arrival, the operations began in the kitchen. Their discipline is very strict, they are fanatics.*
"So, the British have landed?"
"Ten thousand of them. They'll have to have a hundred times more to keep us from throwing them all back into the sea."

Condé, Argentan in ruins.

The night-time settling-in: on the ground floor:

> *living room = Maman, Mademoiselle Martin, Gabrielle [employee of JLRL];*
> *hall = 5 children;*

---

[5] hospital

> *dining room = Grand-maman [paternal grandmother of ELRL] in an armchair.*

Sunday, June 11
During the night, 3 torpedoes in the valleys. Enormous craters, the largest 35 meters around, 4 deep. An ash tree uprooted, 6 poplars decapitated.

Tuesday, June 13
2:30 to 4:30:
Heavy bombings on Caen; we see fires bursting out.
Raoul is very sick and in terrible condition;
occupation and bombings.
No news of the Dufaures. Caen is still on fire. It reaches the spire of Saint Pierre. Dead: Monsieur and Madame de la Hougue, Madame Thomine, Monsieur Ozanne, two children of Doctor Lerasle [people from Caen].
German trucks are camouflaged in the yard; only Mademoiselle Martin's office is occupied. That's the end of our shelters.

Because of the occupation, the night-time settling-in changes:

> *Library = Maman, Mademoiselle Martin, Gabrielle;*
> *Living room = 5 children;*
> *Grand-maman goes back up to her room.*

Wednesday, June 14, 1944
Cannons in the distance. A calm night.
Monsieur de Hédouville [friend of the family] arrives from Caen to get butter and milk in the country. In Caen: Saint-Jean Street is almost extinguished; still more fires on Saint-Pierre Street. There's a question of sending us 50 children, but we need much more by way of accommodations.
In the evening, as usual, trouble in the sky.
Two letters from Uncle Gabriel (Gabriel LRL, older brother of JLRL) transmitted to Levêque (farmer in the village of

Moutiers-en-Cinglais, where the LRLs live) by a courier from Gosselin, are intercepted by the Germans.

Thursday, June 15
2:30 to 3:30 a .m.
Bombardments several kilometers away, glares of the plane's rockets and the explosions of the anti-aircraft.

6 to 7 a.m.
Bombing of Mutrécy and the bridge of the Coudray.
In the afternoon, Maman leaves in an old cart for Harcourt, going a roundabout way. She goes to the Gottards to get butter and eggs for the people in Caen.
By turn, Mademoiselle Martin leaves for la Bagotière to give out the two days' ration of bread to the group of refugees. It's whole grain bread (100 kilos of wheat, 60 kilos of barley, 5 kilos of broad beans, I think). Cashier Madame Lenoury [teacher from the village], Jacqueline Lenoury checks off the cards, Mademoiselle Martin cuts and weighs the bread.

While Maman and Mademoiselle Martin are away, 10 refugees from Couvrechef arrive, breaking down the entrance gate with their handcart. But they excuse themselves for this "little thing" and, as "people of quality," they ask not to be put in with the 10 Gypsy refugees who had arrived at the same time.

Grand-maman draws herself up like Saint Louis rendering justice, and sits on the broken porch. They speak of former household help, family ties.
Grand-maman: "How many children do you have?"
The Gypsy, very amiably: "Let's see, I had ten, I scattered out four on the way. How many does that make?

PREFACE

Originally, I wrote these memoirs only for my family and friends, never imagining that they would be published, especially in the United States. In the beginning, I wanted only to tell entertaining stories, but chapters on the Occupation and Landing were too important to overlook. And yet there is humor even there.

These are snapshots of unforgettable times seen through the eyes of a fifteen-year-old "del Dongo," as in *La Chartreuse de Parme,* where the young hero finds himself in the Battle of Waterloo by accidentally riding into it. After my father's passing, there was a silent agreement that I was head of the family during this unbelievable time, concerned for the welfare of my mother and eleven-year-old sister.

The Liberation brought my first contact with Americans. Because its grandeur has always fascinated me, and distance made it out of reach for such a long time, I decided to devote a complete chapter to the United States. Getting to know Americans was for me a step towards that faraway world that I longed to know.

ARMAND

Chapter I I Was Really Lucky

How can you recapture your oldest memories? Only some old photographs remain, yellowed by time, or the memory of colorful stories heard so often from the mouths of our parents that we recall more from their stories than from actual experiences.

Born one year after the passing of my only brother, Armand, who died of croup at the age of nine, my parents welcomed me as "the miracle child"; but, fearing that I would not be as sweet as the precious one that they had lost, they decided to call me "Albert Jean Armand." Then, after I had, of course, risen in their esteem, they changed their minds, and it was my third first name that became primary. It was also my grandfather's name.

Actually, I have always answered to the two names Albert and Armand, and said "thank you" very politely every time someone wished me Happy Feast Day[6] for one or the other. When I was really little, I was so cute that they also called me "Mimi"! Fortunately, that didn't last long enough to become truly ridiculous. Imagine down at the firehouse: "Have you seen Fireman Mimi"?

My whole life long, to the curious who wanted to know why Albert was also called Armand, I explained pleasantly that the second first name was reserved for the ladies, for it was my mother and my sister who used it most often. Not until much later, having become "Grand-dad," did I think of combining the two first names, more original than Jean-Jacques or Marie-Claude.

Besides my parents, I had a grandmother and Aunt Jeanne to attend to my every need, and I have proof of that. In a photo not taken for that purpose, you can see my little

---

[6] Each day on a French calendar bears a saint's name. In France, one's Feast Day—the Feast Day of the saint whose name you were given—is a bigger occasion than one's birthday, and it is usually complete with gifts and a celebration.

enameled potty inside the open oven door; it was being warmed, to avoid shocking my behind with a cool contact that might make me uncooperative on the potty.

Before my first birthday, I used this hygienic piece of equipment for other purposes: as a first means of self-transportation. Seated and using my legs for locomotion, I could go everywhere, often quickly and unexpectedly—especially if it was for doing mischief, such as going down the cellar stairs. (They wouldn't even let me try!) I already had a taste for travel.

At the age of three, right before Christmas, I had the surprise gift of a little sister. Since I was too young, I wasn't given the choice of a tiny baby or an electric train. At her baptism, I had the feeling that I was no longer going to be the center of the universe, so I tried to keep attention focused on me by endless chatter, and when they would ask me my name, I always answered « Gisèle ». Gisèle was the name of a little neighbor girl, older than I, for whom I must have had tender feelings. They told me that it was impossible because it was a girl's name, but I stuck to it. Didn't I now have to be a little girl like Arlette, in order to hold everyone's interest?

In contrast to my pretty, curly hair that was put up on rollers at night, poor little sister had a skull bald as a pebble. Fortunately, it covered over rather quickly with a down so soft that I loved rubbing it. I couldn't understand why, but she would let loose with howling fits of anger. To justify myself, I said, "I'm not hurting little sister, I'm petting her!"

Sometimes, my parents would point out that I had been really lucky to have been born into a nice home and family. At that age, ignorant of all the laws of nature, I believed that little boys were born in the cabbage patch and that little girls came from roses, so I had to agree that I had been downright lucky.

Yes, I was really lucky! But by the same token, my parents had gotten a really good deal with me!

For my Holy Communion, I received the traditional gifts: From my grandmother, the durable rosary in its case and, from my parents, a superb Mass book on bible paper with gilded edge, and a soft leather cover with my initials etched in chrome-colored metal. My aunt had given me a wonderful silver cover engraved A. I., and our friend Titine's gift was a special intention offering of Sainte Thérèse of the Infant Jesus, painted especially for me on parchment paper by a friend of hers who was a nun.

Among the other gifts, I remember Uncle Emile's: a bicycle pump and a repair kit. He was definitely not a religious person, so I couldn't expect pious gifts, but I loved my Uncle Emile. I had no other uncle and, moreover, he was my godfather.

Uncle Emile was tall, slightly stooped, no longer young, his nose like a pock-marked potato taking up half of his face, a face punctuated with a salt-and-pepper goatee in the style of Napoleon III. He hid his good heart under abrupt manners and a gruff voice—vestiges, no doubt, of his career as a policeman. There are occupations that leave an indelible mark. He also had retained the need for an impeccably clean appearance and meticulous habits of cleanliness, like the brave ritual of washing his bare torso in the morning—in every season of the year—at the outdoor water-pump. He lived in the country, on a poor fixed retirement income, raising rabbits and caring for his garden.

During the war, my mother was not really aware of the danger while the English were firing on the locomotives, and every two weeks she sent me to see Uncle Emile in Audrieu. I took two trains to go fetch a little butter and cream that he had been able to get for us. Usually he treated me to a steak as big as your hand, swimming in blackened butter.

He had become the local policeman appointed by the municipality and, to supplement his income, had agreed to be the telegraph delivery person. At that time, the telephone was still rare and the post office poorly equipped for that purpose. They had simply provided him with a bell that would ring from the P.T.T. [*Poste, Télégraphe et Téléphone*][7] whenever

---

[7] Today, *Poste, Télécommunications et Télédiffusion*: The French post office and expanded communication services.

there was a letter to be delivered. Then he would jump into his old jalopy and set off speeding through the countryside, in all kinds of weather, for many kilometers. The most generous people never failed to thank him with a coin, while the penny-pinchers were content to give him a glass of wine or cider.

One particular day, the messages had sent him out into the heart of the countryside at the base of a hidden valley, in the farm of an old fellow whose home maintenance had been reduced to its simplest form. The chickens gathered up the crumbs and got rid of the flies within reach of their beaks. There was a pervading bitter odor in this room—an odor of fireplaces too immense to be cleaned well—and there was always a little fire glowing in the hearth, smoking and treating hams that were hidden in the stovepipe.

On the immense oak table framed with benches was the traditional carafe of "Calva" [Calvados, apple brandy] and, next to it, a little footed glass, to measure it.

—Hey, Father Emile, you're not going to leave without having a little glass?

—Oh, I can't refuse.

Besides, not accepting would have been an unforgivable insult.

But my uncle was torn between the pleasure of having this drink before going back home, and his distaste for the unique glass that was not only chipped but of a cloudy appearance, announcing that it was never rinsed between visitors. But after all, he had fought in the war of '14 and knew that alcohol disinfects. Having taken hold of the notched side of the glass, he said to himself: "The others couldn't have drunk from this side."

And while he was swallowing his Calva, the old farmer looked at him in surprise and said: "Careful, Father Emile! You could cut yourself. I don't understand, you're drinking exactly like the mailman, from the chipped side."

With time my childhood memories have also curiously broken off. Certain ones live in my memory as clear as if I were seeing them, others are obscured as though in the fog of a dirty glass, and then there are all the others, like shards of shattered glass, of which no memories remain.

Armand, age 5, at the steps of the family home in Caen, 1933

We used to vacation in Douvres, by the sea. On the train from Caen one day, a lady traveler who thought I was a little wild said, "Little girl, you ought to follow the example of your little brother, look how well-behaved he is…!"

When we arrived at the station of Douvres-la-Délivrande, my parents would pass the bags out through the windows of the car, in order to unload them more easily. At times we used to follow the same route, which frightened our cousin

Mercédès a little. She was old enough and big enough to go out through the door.

In 1930, my mother wanted a car, to get to the beach more conveniently, but my parents bought a house there instead. Although it cost as much as a car, the price included some important renovations. The heavy branch of the pear tree had entered a ground-floor window and exited through the roof. This charming pied-à-terre was three kilometers from Brèche Marais, the nearest beach. All we had to do was buy a beach cabana at Luc-sur-Mer, for mid-day picnics and shelter from the sudden downpours that occur there during any season of the year.

Our parents were good enough to push each of us in a baby stroller, so that our little legs wouldn't give out. We conserved our energy for playing on the sand or running between the cabanas with our playmate Jean, in never-ending games of wolf. Sister Arlette, being the youngest, was always the wolf, so that she could never catch us. When she got tired, she just stopped chasing, without letting us know, and we kept running this way and that, like cretins.

On the beach, we would play ball, rings and croquet, and we would organize bass fishing parties. We knew which spots were good for finding periwinkles and mussels, and where we could push the long-handled shrimp net to gather the tiny shrimp of the English Channel. We would seize crabs with our bare hands, using a special technique to keep them from pinching us.

At noontime, we would get our main meal at the meat roaster's shop, on the seafront. I can still see my parents, pulling the cardboard containers out of the bag and setting them on the camping table—containers with slices of roast beef and the sauce that we always poured over them, and the bigger container with the fries. We would eat everything quickly, before it got cold.

The meal was complete with a box of Camembert cheese. To illustrate the healthfulness of the product, the lid pictured a bald monk holding a box of cheese with another monk on it, and I would look past the second, smaller monk to see if there was yet another monk holding a box. This left me open-mouthed with wonder, reflecting on the infinity of the minuscule.

Fishing in *La Manche* [the English Channel].

Every September, it was a family tradition that Aunt Suzanne and her mother, with our cousin Mercedes, came to spend two weeks at our house in Caen. It was a great occasion, marked by a thorough, general housecleaning. We polished the silverware and waxed and polished the dining room, which was hardly used except for those two weeks.

In 1936, Mercedes took advantage of an outing to Douvres to have her hair cut and to have her first permanent wave, as fashion would have it and as her grandmother forbade it. My father had acted as accomplice; with Mercedes staying at his house, he could protect her from her grandmother, who wouldn't have hesitated to slap her, although she was old enough to get herself a fashionable haircut!

Since we went to Douvres only in summertime, the house was not wired for electricity. In September, dinners under the gas lamp or by candlelight brought the family closer and prolonged the pleasure of cracking open the little green crabs called *enragés*, the fruits of the last tide. You had to count on a quarter of an hour to peel one properly without losing a scrap.

We shopped for food at the grocery-café-tobacco shop at the end of the street. The store was managed by Madame Catherine, whose husband had lost a leg at the Chemin des Dames, that particularly bloody strategic site during the final years of World War I. Madame Catherine was a strong woman, with an overflowing bosom and bright red, blotchy cheeks. My father went to her store to pick up his package of shag tobacco. We also bought coffee there, ground to order in a huge machine with a large crank. The whole grinder filled an entire wall space in the little shop.

On the shelves behind the window, the candies in their jars drew us like flies. One contained pink sweets flavored with synthetic strawberry. You had to suck them without biting, or they would break like glass. When our parents said that we could have 100 grams, Madame Catherine dipped them out by the spoonful and weighed them like gold on her Roberval scale, before pouring them into a newspaper cornucopia.

I used to love harvest days in the fields. The mechanical reaper would cut the ears, all assembled in sheaves with hemp rope. Then they were regrouped manually into stacks of five or six sheaves and taken up by pitchfork onto enormous carts, to be put into mills that were as big as houses.

The threshing was even more spectacular, with its steam-driven machine heated with charcoal briquets, like a locomotive. It came clambering up to the mills on wide steel wheels like those of the compressor rollers of railways. It was tied to the thresher by a drive belt, so dangerous that we were warned to keep a good distance.

This "spectacle" unfolded successively in the different farms of the village, where all the men gathered to give a hand. They would pass the sheaves to the farmer on top of the "Machine." He would cut the rope quickly, to leave the ears in a thin layer, in a cloud of dust so dense that his face, eyes protected by motorcycle goggles, was covered in a mask of earth. While they were rebuilding a mill made of de-grained straw, a line-up of carts drove the harvest towards the barns in sacks of 100 kilos, which a single man then managed to carry.

Mid-morning and mid-afternoon, the women would arrive on the work path in a ramshackle cart, with jugs of cider and hefty snacks of bread spread with salted lard or dressed with cold pork—all to keep these kind and generous workers going. At mid-day, they spread out a lavish meal. To get them up on their feet again, it ended with the *jambinette*, coffee laced with Calvados [apple brandy]. You keep topping it off, but only with the Calvados. At the end of the great table, when the master of the house closed up his folding knife with a rough sound, everyone understood the signal and got up and went back to work.

In less than a half-century, Douvres was totally transformed. In the 30's, this peaceful town had been inhabited only by country folk; the peasants were still living by solar time, one hour earlier in summer than official time. They used to complain about the weather, but had found a reason for it. With their strongly accented, truncated syllables, they would say that the T.S.F [*Télégraphie Sans Fils* = wireless radio] waves were to blame for altered weather patterns. On the Bretteville "Path," still not called "Road," the chickens would peck peacefully under the watchful eyes of the roosters, scarcely bothered by the passage of the horses whose manure they were grazing.

Later, that road was paved and connections to city water, electricity and gas were begun, in this two-hundred-year-old town where mice nested in clay walls covered with glued-on plaques. The thatched roofs had not yet been completely replaced by factory tiles—*l'ardoise*, that wavy metal that rusts.

Today, Douvres has become a small suburban area of Caen, in a sense. Some light factories and small malls have even been added. New single homes and housing developments have gone up, and old houses have been modernized. It's another world that the horses, and then the cows, deserted. Some peasants have become rich selling their fields for new construction. And with the automobile, everybody has wheels.

For me, therefore, only memories of my youth in Douvres remain. The children of yesterday have become parents and grand-parents. My friend Joseph is a widower. Ernest now bears an uncanny resemblance to his father: he has exactly the same voice, uses the same characteristic facial expressions. In the front of his mouth, he's also missing three teeth and, like his father, he doesn't feel the need to have them replaced.

CHAPTER II School Days

Maman had already taught me the letters of the alphabet before I started school. I was assigned to the class of the terrible Mrs. Delalande, a stern war widow, very tall, very thin, with a chignon and steel blue eyes that saw every false move. She took to coughing fits and, at certain times, downed medicinal drops which must have been very effective, because she made terrible faces as she swallowed.

There were about forty of us in each class, in somber black aprons, seated on benches in front of inclined desktops, black also so as to show less soil. Knife-carvings showed up brightly. Below was a locker for books and notebooks. On the front of the desk was a small flat section with an elongated hollow for holding pencils, and a hole fitted with a white porcelain ink-holder, which the teacher filled himself with a long-spouted bottle, to avoid spills.

In May, we would gather June bugs and sometimes would attach a little silk paper to them with a string; but most often, we simply freed them in the classroom through a secret maneuver: We would open their box inside the desk, and then remove the inkwell, creating a hole of light so that they could fly out whenever they wanted. Woe to the bug that would take off when the teacher was passing by!

Once, when the windows were open and we had started to release the little critters, the teacher made us shut all the windows—believing that then they couldn't get in, since he logically thought that they had come from outdoors. The result was the opposite, to our great delight.

How happy we were the first day that we were allowed to write in ink with a Sergent-Major pen! You could make spots, ink up the ends of your fingers, or draw a little head on each fingernail... And then, what a good defense method it was against physical punishment: It was enough to grasp the pen-holder firmly in your hand, protecting your face between folded arms, so that the teacher looked twice before giving out slaps.

At snack-time, I had a slice of buttered bread coated with finely grated chocolate. I envied my buddy Hébert, who ate bread with potted pork while he struck sparks by rubbing the sandstone street blocks with his big spiked boots. I longed to wear shoes with nails, too.

Third semester traditionally ended with the awards ceremony. My father, who had studied at the state school of Le Havre, had collected many prizes—superb books gilded on their spines and meticulously kept in the parlor library, from which they were never taken.

At my Catholic school, the books awarded were much more modest. If we nevertheless had many prizes, it was like the Palmes Académiques of Topaze[8]—awarded only for our morals, but tongue-in-cheek.

So it was that on July 17, 1937, I, pupil of the first grouping of *troisième classe,*[9] carried off first prizes for: Politeness, Mental Number Work, Arithmetic, Geography, Good Appearance and Metric System, and second prizes for French History and Grammar. I was very disappointed to note that these eight prizes were reduced to only one skinny little book that I found uninteresting, and that my false crown of paper laurels was painted green only on the outside.

After I had passed these tests, my father enrolled me in the Lycée Malherbe, where I was admitted after a qualifying exam. Since the time of the Napoleonic Empire, the impressive 18th century restored Abbey had been outfitted for the instruction of schoolchildren. I felt intimidated by the routine, the classrooms designated for certain subjects. As soon as the clattering bell was set off by the campus monitor, the pupils would change rooms in joyous commotion. The girls' high school had been appropriated by the occupying Germans, and the concept of co-education was still

---

[8] Topaze is the title and the principal character in a 1928 comedy by Marcel Pagnol. He ridicules the honors (Palmes Académiques) accorded to certain elected officials.

[9] Approximately ninth grade in the United States.

unthinkable, so we had classes only in the afternoon and the girls had classes in the morning.

The French School System & Approximate U.S. Equivalents

Age	France	U.S.A.
	Ecole Maternelle	
2-4	*Petite Section*	Preschool
4-5	*Moyenne Section*	Preschool
5-6	*Grande Section*	Kindergarten
	Ecole Primaire	
6-7	*11è=Cours Préparatoire (CP)*	1st Grade
7-8	*10è=Cours Elémentaire 1 (CE1)*	2nd Grade
8-9	*9è =Cours Elémentaire 2(CE2)*	3rd Grade
9-10	*8è =Cours Moyen 1 (CM1)*	4th Grade
10-11	*7è =Cours Moyen 2 (CM2)*	5th Grade
	Collège	
11-12	*6è =Cycle d'Observation*	6th Grade
12-13	*5è =Cycle'Approfondissement*	7th Grade
13-14	*4è=Cycled'Approfondissement*	8th Grade
14-15	*3è =Cycle d'Orientation*	9th Grade
	Lycée	
15-16	*2nde (Seconde)*	10th Grade
16-17	*1ère (Première)*	11th Grade
17-18	*T (Terminale)*	12th Grade

SOURCE: Giglione, Margaret and Carol Pouchol, eds. *AAWE Guide to Education.* (Paris: AAWE 6th edition, 2003): 198

We had a neighbor named Lamusse, a painter who made a poor living with his Art, along with his devoted sister who, as a youngster, had even served as the model for his painting of the Immaculate Conception. He proposed to give me free lessons in his workshop. Under overhead lighting, this large room was loaded with canvases placed in a disorder understood only to the artist. He settled me before an easel, placed a Canson drawing paper on a cardboard box, and taught me the art of sharpening a piece of charcoal. He said to me: "My young friend, (this was what he called me!) you must hold your charcoal like this, with three fingers, with such light pressure that the Master can, at any moment, pass behind you and remove it without feeling any resistance." Then, while still talking, he executed himself, with ease, what must have been the debut of my studies: "First you will trace, with raised hand, horizontal, parallel lines, then at the next lesson we will go to the verticals, then to the oblique ones in one direction and in the other, after which we will attack curves. Finally, with raised hand, you will draw a perfect circumference where you will mark the center with your eye alone before measuring with the compass the precision of your estimate."

Discouraged by such a program, I never returned to have my second lesson. Perhaps it was a weeding-out process, which allowed him to recognize true future artists worthy of his instruction.

I liked art well enough, but I wanted instant results. So I went to the class of Sister Lefèvre, a Providence nun who painted well. I was content to paint on small pieces of cardboard, my pen dipped in wash. The Allied landing on Normandy's beaches cut short my promising beginnings on the bright path of the Fine Arts, to make of me, in a manner of speaking, an artist victim of war!

When school began in the fall of 1942, I had left the *lycée* [high school] to attend St. Joseph's. It was another world. We had classes all day, with daily testing on the lessons and numerous assignments. The system run by the

Brothers of Christian Schools had a well-deserved, excellent reputation. They were remarkable teachers, capable and dedicated. I owe them everything.

In each class we were taught under the far-reaching gaze of Marshall Pétain, which did not keep the administration from courageously adding to its teachers some members of the Resistance and men who were in hiding to keep from going to Germany.

Since the premises of St. Joseph's institution had been requisitioned by the occupying army, different rooms in town had to be found. The home of the Sisters of Saint Vincent de Paul on *rue de Bayeux* was chosen as base. It was far from our house and, since we no longer could get tires for the bicycles, I replaced the air chambers with old corks, in order to cover the distance. It was a rough ride on the paving stones, but the tires couldn't go flat!

For the first trimester, I had tried taking meals there, but the everyday fare was awful. We ate twelve to a table, in silence. For half of the meal, a reader impressed us with the works of Jean de Larigaudie; it was educational in the "totally boring" genre, and did not help us swallow the blood sausage with rutabaga or with Jerusalem artichokes.

To keep from dying of hunger, the kids from the country who lived at school kept secret reserves in their lockers: butter, jam, potted pork, eggs, etc. Every two weeks, they renewed the supplies by going home to their dear parents. This gave rise to some traffic with the day pupils, who in exchange posted mail directly at the Post Office without going through the censure of the administration. It was a very serious offence, but difficult to detect.

The Principal was known under the nickname "Alcide," to the extent that certain parents called him "Brother Alcide." He was a wonderful man, gifted with an extra-ordinary memory. He knew all the pupils and their families by their first names, even after having seen them only once. He was capable of replacing an absent teacher at the drop of a hat, regardless of the class or subject.

At St. Joe's they attached more importance to math than to languages. So in English we had Brother Levante, who had lived in Great Britain without having acquired the least pedagogical aptitude. He was the only one who was really harassed by the kids.

"Alcide," the beloved schoolmaster and Principal.

One day, when the noise level was so high that you couldn't even hear yourself, he began to blow a whistle like ten city policemen, saying, "Oh, you like noise. I too can raise a ruckus!" A stupefied air of calm took over. Several moments later, the Principal was there, astonished to find a silent, dumbfounded class. The cause-effect was quickly established. We had found a new distraction: whistle for the

Principal, so that he would come see for himself that we were really well behaved.

The second year, Brother Cloarec, "Cloclo" to the pupils (after the character in the comedy *Jean de la lune*), was our main teacher. He had judged it necessary to personally give us an English supplement. It started out with *Practical Words Book*, where the words were grouped by meaning, in two columns per page. We had to learn a new column every day and review five others. He gave us a written quiz every morning, and woe to those who didn't know the words well enough. They had to restudy while walking in the schoolyard during recess. I have retained a huge vocabulary, but its usage is limited by the lack of "inflection"!

After the Liberation, we had "Put Put," a French teacher of Breton origin, which must have explained why for *entièrement* he said *entièrrément*, and for *Atlantique* he ate up the first *t* so that, to our great joy, it became *Alantique*. Since he had noticed all too well our mocking and snickering, he tried to correct himself.

It so happened that they were still setting off mines in the village. One day he wanted to make a point of pronouncing correctly a sentence that he must have carefully prepared in advance: « *Ils traversèrent entièrement l'Atlantique* ». He was answered with a double mine explosion so close by that the windows actually shook. There was an outburst of general laughter and he couldn't help but laugh with us. But he never used those words again; they had unwittingly and unfortunately caused three deaths.

Finally, we arrived at the moment of truth: the famous *baccalauréat.*[10] At each of the sessions from June and

---

[10] A month-long series of exams taken at the end of secondary school. The outcome determines whether the student will achieve free entrance to a university. Considerable extra study is required to pass the *bac*.

September, only 25 per cent of the applicants were expected to pass. At St. Joe's, we succeeded in more than doubling these scores, thanks to our dedicated teachers and to the remedial courses during summer vacation.

In Caen, the *bac* was taken in different classes of the Malherbe High School. There were candidates everywhere, including at the large marble tables of the former monks' dining hall. The pupils were carefully spaced apart from each other. There was strict protocol, identification cards before each student, the black folder with the copies glued shut until the last moment. And the monitors who announced with a certain sadism: "You have no more than a quarter of an hour," or "No more than five minutes."

We had to write with ink pens; some candidates had even brought a second one in reserve. Everybody used a bottle of Waterman ink to refill the rubber cartridge. After the second part of the exam, the kids were letting off some steam, and broke an inkbottle on the white pedestal of the statue of Louis XIV dressed as a Roman emperor. At that time, it decorated Marronniers Square in front of the lycée.

I have no memory of my exams. I was so tense that I couldn't eat anything that day. For questions from our courses, we could choose among three subjects; since there was a little book called *The Annals of the Baccalauréat*, with all the tests of the previous years in all the Academics, I had found one of the three. I had focused on only ten or so questions in each subject. Which avoided burdening my mind for final reviews.

I remember one very embarrassing question in the oral English exam: "Let's see, did you have a bad English teacher, or didn't you work?" I thought it clever of me to answer modestly: "Oh, no sir, I had a good English teacher and I worked a lot all year, but I don't have a good ear." I thought it was better to blame my ear rather than my mind. That's how I avoided a really bad grade.

GRADE EQUIVALENCIES

(French grades are based on 20 possible points; e.g.,14/20.)

FRANCE		U.S.A.
19, 20		A+
18, 17	"A" range: = excellent, very good	A
16		A-
15		B+
14, 13	"B" range: = good	B
12		B-
11		C+
10	"C" range: = average	C
9		C-
8, 7		D+
6	"D" range: = below average	D
5		D-
4, 3, 2, 1	"F" range: = failing	F

(Ghiglione & Pouchol 2003, 198)

CHAPTER III THE OCCUPATION

Television didn't exist as yet, only big radio receivers with tubes with plenty of sound interference. We had no radio at home, so that we wouldn't be distracted from our studies. Newspapers were censored by the government, to keep the citizens calm. Sometimes when an entire article was taken out, it left a big white space, but there was no discount for the paper—we just bought it and imagined what it might have said.

In this beautiful month of May 1940, the news was not so great. We opposed the rapid advance of the German armies with "the elastic defense," the extraordinary war tactic of backing up constantly, so as to draw the enemy further from their bases and make them more vulnerable. We could then surround them more easily and divide them into smaller sections.

This also explained the arrival of more and more refugees. They started coming from the right bank of the Seine, and then didn't feel safe in Normandy because they felt too exposed. When they preferred to continue towards the South, we began to wonder: weren't we ourselves going to become the refugees of tomorrow?

Then, the following Sunday, the sky turned blacker than we had ever seen it, so black that we had to light the kitchen lamp at noontime. It was clouds without rain, clouds that dropped fine, greasy dust that stuck everywhere. Our French Army had burned the oil reserves of Le Havre and Ouistreham, to cut off the feeding line for enemy advancement.

The next day, an old dirty soldier asked for civilian clothing, to go home to Thury Harcourt, south of Caen, and avoid being taken prisoner. Was he deserting? He left us his regulation gear: a cap, an empty water flask and a pair of cartridges. He never came back, and we wondered if he had been shot.

With strategic counter-moves, the SNCF[11] had chartered a railcar to evacuate administrators and their families towards Brittany. We were allowed only one suitcase, but I had added a salad basket full of cherries, a souvenir from the garden. I asked my mother, "What will we do with the basket afterwards?" She answered, "We'll throw it out—it's not important." Because we were always so economical at home, I anguished terribly over this answer. Was the situation so desperate that we could throw away a perfectly good salad basket?

After an unbelievable train trip, avoiding bridges destroyed too soon by the military engineers, we arrived in Avranches. There we saw an English convoy pass by; it appeared to be re-embarking from another site. At that moment, a German plane fired on it. This was the first time that I saw a Stuka with black crosses. The English hurried off into the low sides of the road.

Arlette, at the age of eight and a half, had been surprised by this unexpected baptism of fire, and was crying noisily. We took shelter in a little shack nearby, afraid of a new attack. Then, according to a maternal tradition, Mother wanted to have the little one urinate, to calm her childish fears, because "she had been so frightened." Except that the lavatory was at the far end of the yard—in the line of fire—and, since there wasn't even a chamber-pot, she had to accomplish this in an unforgettable blue-flowered salad bowl, left on the table since the mid-day meal. The plane didn't come back, the English left, and so did we, in search of lodging for the night.

It was Madame Micoin-Saint-Saëns, the grand niece of the great composer, who agreed to keep us. She must have thought us quite clean and polite, and preferable to some

---

[11] *Société Nationale des Chemins de Fer Français*: The French rail system, including but not limited to the *métro* [subway], its extended lines outside of the center of Paris, high-speed trains throughout France, and the Eurostar under the English Channel to London.

strangers that the mayor could have officially imposed on her in the big house where she lived alone.

We were on the lookout for all the news, but it was contradictory. It seemed that old Marshal Pétain had been charged with signing the Armistice, and that a rebel General [De Gaulle] was calling for a continuation of the war from England, where he was inviting them to join in. Rumor now had it that the enemies were already in Rennes, and were going to occupy all of France. Therefore, it was useless to continue westward, so the autorail simply took us back to Caen.

The house had not been looted, and in town we didn't find much that was different. I saw my first two Germans in a motorcycle with sidecar, wearing funny brimless headgear and the large *Feld-grau* ["battlefield gray"] raincoats, which must have made them sweat. The *Kommandantur* [Headquarters] had already been moved into the Hotel Malherbe, the biggest and the best in the city. From its façade hung two large, vertical red flags embellished in their centers with the famous *Swastika*. On the city walls, they had just pasted yellow, bilingual posters, dictating the orders of the occupying army.

To begin with, they required us to turn in all arms, under penalty of being shot. Since the Germans were well organized, and since they wanted to see how we were accepting them, they had taught the soldiers the question to ask methodically in each house in the city: *Havez-vous des Harmes ?* [Do you have any arms]?

Alas, the pronunciation left something to be desired, and Bousset, a poor old gentleman living across from us, somehow thought he should answer yes, so as not to upset the soldier. My father, who had occupied the Ruhr in 1919 [World War I], explained that the old man was a little deaf and that he was not too bright. Fortunately for Father Bousset, the affair went no further.

I then learned that we ourselves had a small-cylinder revolver in the house. It was out of the question to turn it over to the enemy; we were not going to contribute to their arms! Dad wrapped it in a greasy rag before placing it in one of those old cylindrical, all-purpose sugar boxes. He then hid it under the great pile of coal, generously bought a month earlier to help our coal vendor move his stock. This was a wise move that would provide us with some warmth during the whole war.

At that time, we would go every day to the neighborhood grocery for fresh milk, and bring it back in an aluminum can. The can was fitted with a handle that could be turned vertically, so that the milk miraculously did not spill. That day, in the shop, there was a superb German officer in bouffant culottes and high cap, even more important-looking because he was buying beautiful peaches. Very kindly, he offered a splendid one to my little sister. He insisted and she continued to refuse, but the grocer made her accept it. "It's offered so nicely!" he said. Perhaps the officer was a father who would have enjoyed giving it to his own daughter…

I can still picture Arlette, that good little woman, furious that she had been forced to take the fruit. She had barely cleared the front of the store when she threw the peach to the ground, saying: "For sure it's poisoned; a German gave it to me." I already had a practical mind and didn't care where the peach had come from, so I hurried to devour it.

Then my parents, to teach me a lesson and highlight the heroic refusal of the food-loving little girl, started to agree that the fruit had to be poisoned. As I began gradually to believe them—for they usually didn't lie to me—I turned whiter and whiter shades of pale. They had to stop their bad joke, which would have ended with me really getting sick, and perhaps dying by way of power of suggestion!

But this "good" time was not to last; soon we had ration coupons, which were then replaced by all sorts of combinations. I was astonished to learn how a grocer "watered down" milk; it already seemed very naturally watery to me. They also said that boxes of sugar pieces were no longer full. When I remarked on it to the grocer lady, she explained learnedly—to hide her theft—that this sugar had become so precious that the manufacturers were now weighing the packets one by one. I thought that it must have been quite a job for them!

Sometimes, we learned that with the "TZ" or "XY" ticket, you could get something, such as pasta or jam. We always bought it, even if we didn't need it right away, because we could eventually use it. I still remember the strange feeling when my mother brought home a bowl that I thought was full of fruit sauce, and I dipped my finger all the way in before noticing that it was hot mustard!

There were secret exchanges, such as when we gave our tobacco tickets to a peasant friend who gave us wheat to feed our chickens. Then I took the hen's eggs to school and exchanged them for sugar. Shoes, clothing, all merchandise was difficult to obtain. It was the time when you found shoes at the butcher shop and sausages at the shoemaker's. The important thing was to know the right address and have an exchange coupon.

The authorities dealt severely with anyone caught dealing in the black market, where you could get whatever you wanted for a higher price. We never bought anything on the black market, because it was dishonest. Besides, we didn't have much money! Poverty kept us honest!

For something special, we sometimes made crepes. We had to grind up the grain in a coffee grinder, which got more and more stubborn. Usually, we decided not to sift the flour, so that it made more. We still had to crush chunks of sugar on a board with a bottle because, for some unknown reason, our poor rations were always supplied in pieces. Then we got the idea of depositing the sugar on the crepe following a line, which served as the guide for rolling it. This was the best way to be sure of finding a little sugar in each mouthful.

Everything we bought was taxed. The nice farmer neighbors from the house in Douvres agreed to sell us potatoes, but we had to go get them. On each trip, Mom brought back a filled baby carriage on foot, to avoid being picked up by the economic control.

And I, each time that I would go to see my friend François Le Roy Ladurie in Montiers-en-Cinglais, would always bring back a little butter and cream that they sold us at the cost of the tax—but it was a long trip by bicycle!

Despite everything, it was decided to organize a family get-together for Arlette's Holy Communion. My mother had raised a sheep with her coffee tickets; that is, for six months, she gave her coffee tickets to the Mayor of Ifs, who, on the given date, supplied her with a sheep. Imagine the party for all those bellies starved for meat.

Unfortunately, nothing could be kept; freezing was not yet available to the public. Therefore, Maman suggested sharing the meat to a discrete neighbor, the mother of a large family. The neighbor refused because she had just returned from Brittany after the death of her mother-in-law, and suddenly having meat would have suggested the unthinkable to the imagination.

At that time, we were like the majority of the French—partisans of Marshal Pétain, whose personality cult had been carefully developed. Was he not our only defense against the occupying Army? His photographs on post cards had been widely distributed. His portrait on posters decorated every official place and even every classroom. Was it not he who arranged distribution of vitamin-enriched casein cakes at each recess? I didn't like them, and re-sold them to my friends so that I could buy saccharin ice creams from Gomez's cart at the end of the main courtyard. *A chacun son goût!* [To each his own!]

For several months, my friend François' father had been Minister of Agriculture in Vichy, long enough for him to take a very popular measure: he gave a pound of bread per day to the farmers, on the premise that those who were producing the wheat ought not to be without it. This measure was, as so many others, a smokescreen. It was obvious that the peasants had always secretly furnished wheat to their baker, who was freely giving them bread.

Beyond bread and other necessities of life, everything was in short supply, leading to some bizarre measures. Workers pulled old nails from buildings, to straighten and reuse them. For ammunition, the Germans salvaged every bronze statue, with one exception that I learned of: the equestrian statue of Napoleon Bonaparte, pointing a scornful finger across the Channel towards England.

The Germans had requisitioned houses, and took up residence. Downtown, they could be seen parading impeccably, while singing the famous « *Aï! Aio !* » Their Supply Corps moved along in humble, common horse-drawn carts. They had strange tanks, whose sides were narrower at the bottom than on top, and they were equipped with four wheels, of which the first two pivoted, but the two poor nags pulling them seemed more suited to the farm than the conquering Army.

To "protect" us, big projectors and batteries of German anti-aircraft defense were positioned on the city's high points. The alert sirens sounded three sinister roars to announce the arrival of the planes of the "enemies," our allies of yesterday. We would have had to go to the public shelters, with white paint on the outside doors showing the number of persons that they could hold; but since we didn't live downtown, we stayed at home when the sirens sounded.

By day, we counted the planes passing, and we saw them framed by lightning bolts followed by little black clouds, the firings of the German anti-aircraft defense. A moment afterwards, we would hear the explosions reverberating in scattered fashion on the rooftops and flooring. It was no time to be out in the yard. Like other children, I hurried out afterwards to gather up these still-burning war souvenirs, which I have kept ever since.

By night, the passage of the planes brought another spectacle: the enormous parallel beam projectors striping the sky with giant, luminous paintbrushes, searching out targets among the clouds. Woe to anyone found in their rays. All the artillery would open—a real fireworks display, with streaming explosions and ricocheting bullets, a Fourteenth of July[12] complete with firecrackers. Curiosity and our lack of experience allowed us to brave out this dangerous show.

---

[12] The anniversary of the storming of the Bastille, French Independence Day.

Later, we would see hundreds of flying fortresses—the big bombers—surveying us at 30,000 feet, leaving white condensation trails. Sometimes the *Flag* (German aircraft defense) greeted them with cannon bursts. They held to their perfect straight-line formation, going further on to drop the bombs.

Sometimes the Allied bombers dropped pamphlets that we were obliged to deliver to the *Kommandantur* without reading them. Of course, we did the opposite. The Americans sent us little newspapers in A4 format [8½"x 11"], folded in half. The English sent sheets of paper covered very closely with tiny lettering. Knowing nothing of the printing process, I marveled at how printers could be so skillful as to assemble such tiny characters.

They also dropped odd little bands of paper, metallic on one side and black on the other. All sorts of stories circulated about them—they could have been secret messages that special ink would have revealed. Some people tried unsuccessfully to boil them. We had no way of knowing that their purpose was practical—to interfere with radar images, the very existence of which was unknown to us.

Only at the time of Liberation did I see the remains of gigantic radar stations in Douvres in the *blockhaus*,[13] and the recovery of drawers of electronic material; but the Germans had carefully destroyed the transformers with their revolver shots, before turning them over.

No doubt to avoid suspicion as to the landing site, Caen had been lightly bombed during the Occupation, so that when we—for reasons unclear to me—decided to visit Rouen, we were upset to see the state of destruction of the heart of the city, where the spires of the cathedral stood out. That was our first contact with a badly damaged city, and we had but one wish: to return home as quickly as possible. But

[13] One of the small, defensible buildings that the Germans built, partially in the ground, for defense and as a firing point for their soldiers.

we had to wait the whole day, in anguish, for the only evening train.

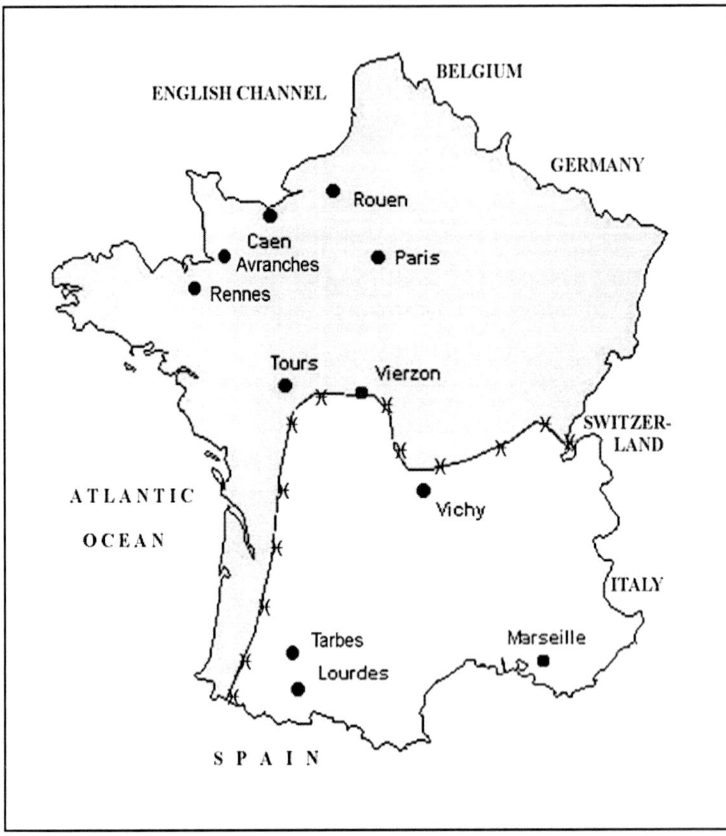

France in 1942, showing the demarcation line between the Occupied zone (gray) to the north and the "Free" zone to the south.

On another occasion, despite everything, we wanted to make a pilgrimage to Lourdes. This was no better an idea. Around midnight, a while before arriving at the demarcation line of Vierzon and entering the free zone, our tickets were checked on the train by a German policeman. We learned that we should have had a date stamp put on our card, at the police station. The policeman made us get off the train, and abandoned us on the platform. After trying to procure this date stamp at the window of the police station—closed, of course, at that late hour—we finished the night in the station waiting room. There, in the early morning, a kind railroad worker authorized our cards with a false stamp, allowing us to continue en route to our devotions. The Holy Virgin took pity on us.

A certain Resistance had been organized, especially after the denunciation of the German-Soviet pact. Up to then, the Communists had been rather partisan [devoted to their Communist party], like Thorès who deserted, or like Marchais, who went to work in Germany. After Germany invaded Russia and the pact was denounced, they received orders to join in the French Resistance, in hopes of establishing Communist power in France at the Liberation.

To avoid sabotage of the rail lines and telecommunication cables that the Germans had installed along the tracks, the cities had to organize "swing shifts" so that security-cleared men could keep night watch over the lines after their day work. If it came to it, the Resistants had to take them along, or tie them up and gag them before carrying out their sabotage, so that they wouldn't be shot as accomplices.

In the daylight, planes were machine-gunning locomotives, to cut down on depot hauling. For defense, the convoys were accompanied by a flatcar fitted with four twin tubes of small, 20 mm cannons. We could see the unfortunate soldiers, numb from the cold and the high speed, looking for the enemy in the sky—the enemy ready to swoop down on them, the enemy that they were obliged to fight.

The mechanics had a cruel choice: either join the underground and leave their families without means of support, or continue to serve as a target. To reassure them, they had been provided with several sheets of metal plating on the back of the cab, which theoretically protected them. Some were scalded by the locomotive boiler when it was pierced by bullets. A long list was posted on the station wall, naming the region's railroad workers who had been killed on the job.

To prevent sabotage of trains carrying their soldiers on leave, the Germans thought of adding a car of French officials just behind the engine. The officials had been offered a free round trip ticket beyond the Rhine, but these short, spur-of-the-moment tourist trips were not popular.

Offers of employment in factories in Germany, supposedly to help free prisoners of war, had little success, and some young people joined the underground Resistance.

In the marshalling yards, resistant railroad workers were completing special boxes with sand for the railroad cars—boxes which, after rolling along for a moment, would become red-hot and set off breakage of the axle, derailing the train.

To head off clandestine landings, the Germans had planted "Rommel asparagus" in the fields. Imagine pyramids made of three platform foundations joined at their heads and tied together at the base. Unfortunate citizens trying to position themselves in the grass to free spies or rescue Allied pilots would be wiped out. Later, in the harvest season, the practical peasants would dry their grain there.

Gradually, the town was decorated with carefully placed blockhouses, waiting for the necessary guns and ammunition to arrive. Located a distance apart in the soil, scooped-out hollows for land mines lay ready for just the right moment. On certain streets, enormous metallic doors were erected to stop the tanks in their tracks.

It was generally during the milkman's hour that plainclothes police in raincoats and soft hats discretely gathered up the Resistants and the Jews in their homes. They were taken away in black front-wheel drive automobiles. That's how we saw them take the militant Communist who lived very close to us.

As so many others, we also had our Jewish person to hide, but we had to return her rather quickly to those who had entrusted her to us, because she couldn't remain quiet and out of sight. She insisted on walking in the daytime in the garden, where she was visible from the apartment building next door.

Armand, age 14, Nov. 1942

We were never decorated for that heroic deed, and I was still too young to be part of the Resistance and too pacifist to be tempted by it. But I did help a friend who wanted to enter the Movement, by giving him the famous barrel pistol, which he fortunately never had to use, because the barrel—which my Dad must never have greased—was so rusted that it just might have blown off his hand if he had fired it.

The occupying soldiers knew that, despite their ban and the risks, everyone was listening to the BBC [British Broadcasting Company], to access reliable news and to catch the mysterious personal messages. The messages included announcements of parachute drops of equipment for the different underground branches. It ended with them confiscating all the radio sets in our region, ordering that they be deposited in the town halls. The only radios kept belonged to cheats who had avoided the tax by not declaring them. Their risk was serious: deportation.

I remember a rebellious citizen who, so that his radio couldn't be used, had attached a leash to it and pulled it on a sidewalk before turning it over to the Special Service in the city. Mademoiselle Fumichon, Arlette's teacher, had recently acquired a superb set, in order to hear the English better, but since it had been declared, she found herself obliged to turn it over. Luckily, I had an old set that had been assembled in a crate at the beginning of the century, and I gave it to her to declare as a substitution. So hers was spared from the fire in city hall, where all the others went up in flame on the evening of June 6, 1944.

BBC broadcasts were received on several different short wave frequencies. Usually one of them—never the same—had less interference than the others. That was the one that the Germans wanted to hear.

It was Radio Paris that let us know about the landing in Dieppe. This time it was for real, but the English were put back to sea, with fury and great losses.

Later, I met a French-speaking Canadian who had lost his sergeant's stripes. He was in the second wave of landings and, seeing the fate of friends who had gone before him, responded to his English officer, "Well, buddy, if you want to land, go right ahead." And after having put this courageous but foolhardy officer over the side, he made a half-turn with their boat. Later, he was only put in prison and de-commissioned; they needed men too badly to shoot him.

Life became much more difficult as time went on, both in finding the necessities of life and in getting along with the occupying army. We heard more and more talk of Resistants being shot, imprisoned or deported. The situation had come to a head, and there seemed no way out other than an Allied invasion. Although we were only fourteen years old, my friend François Le Roy Ladurie and I tried a little strategizing: This fervently-wished-for landing, where could it take place? After the failure in northern France, where the coastline had to be particularly well defended by the Germans, what remained across from England? Le Contentin was too narrow. Brittany, a little wider, was nevertheless too far to provide a battlefield. Our conclusion was not a happy one: It seemed obvious that Calvados was the ideal place for this heroism to take place.

During one of these conversations, I confessed to François that we would have no place to take refuge during that landing. Without hesitating, he said, "In that case, you'll come to our place in Villeray." When the Allies landed about where François and I had predicted—very close to home—my father was no longer with us. He had died of a heart attack in 1942. In an unspoken agreement, my distraught mother and I decided together what would become of us. I never forgot François' words, and we did eventually leave our home in Caen and present ourselves at the Château. There we were welcomed with open arms, to spend with them those unforgettable days from the Landing to the Liberation.

CHAPTER IV THE LANDING

At La Bagotière, the German soldiers had hung branches of lime trees to camouflage their trucks and tanks. The drying leaves gave off a bitter smell that I still recognize among all other scents. After so many years, I remember that odor, mixed with the lingering smell of battle powder and the sweat of exhausted men. Then my mind moves to the picture of the men covered with ochre-colored dust from the gutted paths.

For me, the perfume of the dying foliage is all that. All that and much more, from the first day of the landing, June 6, 1944, when the roaring of the Navy artillery had begun at dawn, like a gigantic and distant storm. Could this really be The Landing? The joy and the agony, were they indeed meant for us?

After the raid at 1300 hours, the streets were blocked with razed houses, German reinforcements no longer had access, and entire families left Caen. They passed in front of our house to go into hiding in the old subterranean stone quarries in Fleury-sur-Orne. Some left in a crazed state, taking nothing with them. Perhaps they had already lost everything? Others were loaded down with bicycle trailers and little kids' carts packed with bizarre, mixed-up piles of mattresses, coverlets, and other various items. —What? There was a child pulling a cage of canaries. A grandmother was moaning in a wheelbarrow pulled by her son-in-law, his head collared and held steady in a strap.

Along their passage, these fleeing persons were hanging onto broken telephone lines, spread out in tangles on the ground. They invented new passages, avoiding the bomb craters and the hills of debris. Under the destroyed houses, they sometimes thought that they heard the weak voices of those buried inside.

With old tables, I had made a simple shelter in the henhouse. This actually was an even more dangerous refuge, but we would go there to spend the night and get through a long bombing. We had the idea that they would try to destroy the railroad bridge at the foot of the cliff below our house. The planes came in successive waves. After four passes dropping bombs, they made an observation tour, and the waltz towards the still-standing metal bridge began anew. Four small bombardment runs and one bomb-less run, during the hours of one endless night. We could see in the yard as though it were daylight; it was illuminated with a strange apocalyptic light shining curiously from the north. This was the whole city burning, its red flames reflected on clouds of smoke. Little fake suns hung from small parachutes, lighting up this unreal decor with magnesium whiteness and outlining the bombing zones.

Sometimes the bombs came from very high, whistling with infinite slowness; at other times, they arrived in quick, screeching breaks, making us instinctively draw our heads into our shoulders. The explosions became deliverances, shaking us from head to foot like gravel in a sieve. We weren't dead yet! We mistakenly believed that the volley of blows coming to us then were no more than amusing showers of metallic hailstones.

Finally, it was calm. We collapsed with fear and fatigue. When we awoke, it was full daylight and the house was still standing. But since we had left the windows open to keep them from breaking, the house seemed to look at us with great sunken eyes. The railroad bridge was still intact. Was it all just a frightful nightmare?

No, it was real, because the wind still carried the bitter odor of flying cinders with half-charred ends of papers, and the calm was punctuated with the frightening sound of crumbling houses. From the street came the confused murmur of a phantom-like procession of fleeing, shaggy-haired individuals, including the wounded, lightly bandaged with already-dirty rags. They were leaving, going they knew not where. And the dogs, all the dogs in the city, answered each other, howling at death.

Yes, they had really landed—the immense Armada beating the beaches baptized with new names: Sword, Juno, Omaha, Utah. Paper decrees dropped from the sky and ordered us to leave, saying that our city was now condemned!

Mother and I agreed that the grave dangers on the road seemed safer than staying in our home. Nothing to be done but reduce our affairs to one load and run towards the uncertain future. Would we come back one day? Would we see our house again? Before leaving, I yielded to the impulse to bury our last two, old bottles of Médoc[14] in the yard. I spotted each with a stone, but we were never to find either bottle. Did they furnish the last pleasure of the nameless soldier who left his blood on our staircase? Did they fortify the bomb disposal experts when they came by?

By noon, we were fleeing towards Les Moutiers-en-Cinglais, pushing our old, filled-to-overflowing baby carriage. Rather than agonize over whether to take the works of Dante or Shakespeare, we were more practical and chose the last jar of blackberry jam. Holding Arlette, Mother and I relayed on the single bicycle. Towards evening, exhausted from a trip of 25 kilometers,[15] we reached the road to the Château de Villeray. Horrors! A column of German reinforcements was hidden under the trees. We were blocked, and forced to complete the trip with a detour of three kilometers, which seemed the longest part of the journey.

Our friends, the Le Roy Ladurie family, welcomed us warmly and gave us a room on the second floor, where we moved in before dinner. That evening, there was a marvelous dessert of wild strawberries, the first of the season. Right from the first day, we were part of the family. Maman helped in the kitchen, and I shared garden chores with my friend François. We began by mulching the strawberry plants with straw.

---

[14] Bordeaux wine made in the Médoc region.

[15] One kilometer = 5/8 of a mile.

Omaha Beach today, with the English Channel at low tide

Before noon, the first bomb arrived and broke the château windows. I was thrown to the ground nose first in the yard, and the impact stopped my pocket watch, a treasured gift from my father. It was 11:20 a.m. We swept up the broken panes in the house—shamefully, as if we were at fault, as if bad luck had followed us there.

At the château, where the ways of the city meant nothing, life had maintained a decorum to which we were unaccustomed. Gabrielle, the cook, announced the meals with the bell. At the first ring, we had to come in from different points of the estate to wash up and change. At the second ring, we went to the dining room and waited behind our chairs until Grandmother Le Roy Ladurie was seated. Then we all sat, and she played out her role as mistress of the house.

She was a tall and noble lady, dressed all in black, and very proud to say that each of her three sons measured not less than 1 m 85 [1 meter 85 centimeters] in height. She moved about with difficulty, with the help of a silver-capped cane. Around her neck she wore this little band of black velvet; among the aristocrats, it was meant to hide the mark of the guillotine, my father had told me as a joke. Although I never believed in this macabre make-believe, I secretly entertained the thought that without that black velvet band, her head would fall off and we might see traces of glue.

Her fear of modern war methods was equal only to her courage. We were all at the dining room table at the time of the terrible bombardment that annihilated Evrecy. So that we could not see fear drain the color from her face, she said with much dignity, while hiding her head under her napkin: "This way, my children, if I die, you will not have to see my disfigurement."

Despite her youth, Cécile, François's little sister, tried with her comments to comfort my poor mother, who was demoralized by the circumstances. She affectionately called her « *Maman Idrac* ».

Château de Villeray, where the Idracs first took shelter during the Landing. Today, descendants of the Le Roy Ladurie family own the property.

At Villeray, generosity was limitless; often, they received people from Caen en route to distance themselves even further from the battlefield. One day, Monsieur Etterlé passed by with his whole family. He was a well-known and important entrepreneur of public works in Caen. With age, and perhaps for some other reason, his voice had become frighteningly deep, and he said to me: "Do you hear those cannons beyond the valley of the Orne?" I had grown accustomed to the sound of the cannon fire, but not yet to the sound of his sepulchral voice, which reminded me later of Malraux in his speech on Jean Moulin.[16]

Sometimes we thought we heard a train passing on the abandoned line from Caen to Flers; it sounded like rattling rails, with the valley responding in echo. But it was really a convoy of tanks hurtling down the sunken lane extending from the other side of the Orne towards coast 112, which had to be taken and retaken so many times.

[16] Jean Moulin (1899-1943), a French Resistant born in Béziers and buried in the Panthéon in Paris in 1965.

Ironically, we were near the battlefields but knew nothing at all of the battle outcomes. Transistor radios were not yet invented; we had one crystal set that worked without current, but the sound was very weak and it was difficult to regulate. Of course, there were no newspapers.

During the Occupation, we used to receive occasional pamphlets from planes passing overhead, but now the Allies no longer took the time to give us their news. All we could do was attempt translations of the information bulletins that the Germans posted at their camp entrances. Even while doubting their credibility, we would find names of towns we knew, and tried to figure out where the Allies were advancing.

During a period of calm, we would go onto a high area near National Route 162. In clear weather, we could make out the area of Caen, where columns of black smoke were climbing high into the sky, and in cloudy weather we saw the streaks of cannon fire. But these morbid sights told nothing more.

In Caen, enormous red crosses had been painted on the rooftops of the Church of St. Steven, the Lycée Malherbe and the dwelling of the Little Sisters of the Poor, where civilians and wounded had found refuge. After the bombings, every able man—including youngsters as young as I—were charged with searching for the wounded and the dead among the ruins. They evacuated the wounded and set aside the dead, for burial.[17]

The needs of the civilians in Caen were becoming urgent. Madame Le Roy Ladurie tried to organize a convoy of wheat for them, but no one in the village dared venture onto the road with a wagon and horses. She declared that if it came to that, she herself would go on June 22nd, so several men were

---

[17] Late in August, when we returned to Caen, I remember certain streets at the foot of the Château of William the Conqueror, as well as in the center of town, where the ruins were two to three meters high. The foul odor of decaying cadavers was to last for several months.

shamed into going with her. We left with shoulder lanyards full of sacks of wheat. I went along to see the state of our house, and to try to bring back a change of clothing, which was badly needed.

The morning that we set out, the weather was overcast, with low clouds that seemed to dodge machine-gun fire. Before Laize-la-Ville, a long German ammunition convoy had exploded and burnt; at the edge of the road, the sheet metal trucks—already rusted—gave off groaning and grinding noises at the lightest breeze. Cartridges of all kinds were spread on the ground; they would have made a great souvenir collection, but I held so little hope of surviving that I did not gather any.

After having seen so many houses destroyed, I was really worried about ours. Oh joy! It was almost intact, hardly ransacked. I gathered some clothes into an old potato sack, and then rejoined the handcarts at the home of the Little Sisters of the Poor. For the return trip, they had already loaded several bags of salt, which would later allow us to preserve the meat of animals killed in the war.

In the afternoon, the weather was very pleasant, and the bombings had started anew. On the route to Falaise,[18] at the exit from Caen, enormous craters blocked passage even more so than the artillery with its random bursts of gunfire.

The road to Harcourt seemed calm by comparison, but the towns of Saint-Martin-de-Fontenay and May-sur-Orne were already completely destroyed. In Saint-Martin, a cabaret owner had set up a sort of café under the ruins of sheet-metal roofing from his house. Out of consideration for her "working crew," and following the rules of etiquette, Mme Le Roy Ladurie offered a *café-calva* [coffee with apple brandy] to everyone. Only Père Lemarrois, who didn't like to drink, claimed to be in a hurry and continued on the road.

---

[18] The birthplace of William the Conqueror, Duke of Normandy, who defeated Henry II in the Battle of Hastings (1066).

His bay horse was pulling a covered wagon bearing a white flag of truce.

During our stop at the bistro, we had heard a short machine-gun burst. Alas, on the road at the end of town, we found Lemarrois. His horse and he were dead, the wagon riddled with bullets, torn to pieces despite the pathetic white rag hanging on its pole of shattered hope. The poor man was beyond our help.

The next challenge was to clear the valley of the Laize. There was a steep decline before the bridge, followed by a rather rough coastline—a site where it had been hoped to attack the convoys, with planes that surveyed the route constantly. Curiously, that was where, long ago, bandits used to attack carriages.

We managed to pass this place between two volleys of bullets. On the downgrade, we were thrown into the trench. I can still see Mme Le Roy Ladurie lying in the grass in front of me, holding her big pocketbook against the nape of her neck. For her, this was the most essential point to protect. Since I didn't have a pocketbook, I couldn't imitate her, so I simply crossed my fingers on my skull, hoping to protect my brains!

By pulling back, the Germans were chasing farmers, settling and then fighting from their lands. That was how Victor came to us. He was a small farmer from nearby, who had quickly rediscovered the response of his ancestors to stress: seek the help of the *Seigneur*.[19] His exhausted old horse pulled up with the family and a few old clothes in a tipcart, and his four cows taking up the rear. Poor Victor was so upset when he entered with this entourage that he noisily overturned a front gate support—unfortunate entrance when asking for shelter. He tried to explain to Grandmother, who generously and loudly assured him: "My poor man! We can replace it." It was the best that she could say.

They were allowed to bed down in the barn, joining the group of refugees already there. Victor was energetic, and

---

[19] From feudal times: the lord and master of the estate.

had offered his help, so they put him to work using steel wool on the parquet flooring of the château. Dying of the heat, and with no regard for the nobility of the place, he took off his shirt. When my friend saw him, he couldn't resist the temptation to hide the shirt. And soon we heard the poor devil running through the château hollering, "Someone stole my shirt, my only shirt!"

Then the Germans decided to turn Villeray into a country hospital. All refugees had to leave, since they would tolerate only the owners. For a few days, they placed us in an abandoned village house; then we found refuge with Raymonde, guardian of the Château de la Bagotière, who was too afraid of the troops to sleep in his own home. It was there that we saw the German army up close. They occupied the entire château, hiding the automatic machine-gun in the park area. These shock troops[20] could be denied nothing.

One day, a young SS officer amused himself in front of the children by putting their little cat in the mouth of his German shepherd. Granted, the dog didn't hurt it, but the children were screaming with fright and the poor little animal was terrorized. What was the point of this cruelty, when we could all die tomorrow? At any given moment, they might come into the house to ask for butter, eggs or "milk cream." Since we had no inclination to serve them, they didn't hesitate to take out a persuasive pistol. We learned not to be afraid, just to open the empty cupboard doors, and they would leave with no problem, sometimes discharging the pistol on the weathervane of the compass card, for no real purpose.

I still think of those men, who one last evening before mounting the attack were harmonizing so melodiously in the park—singing *lieds* [German songs for solo voice and piano]

---

[20] Members of the military especially suited and chosen for offensive work because of their high morale, training and discipline.

of their country, accompanying themselves with harmonicas. I never saw any of them come back.

It was during that time that they set up three enormous 220 mm cannons in the woods of la Hoguette, 300 meters from where we were staying at the Château de la Bagotière. The cannons would all fire at the same time, setting off a terrible shaking of the house. On the walls, the great *oeil de boeuf*[21] and the picture frames jumped, ready to fall, and all the dishes clattered in the buffet cabinet. The artillery of the Allies answered. We heard the shots initiate, and we recognized the responding batteries by their sound.

Sometimes we could even see a high explosive shell pass like a shadow. By their whistle, we could distinguish those that would go further from those that would land nearby.

We ended up getting used to it all!

Every day, we would go see our friends in Villeray, but that meant passing near the battery of la Hoguette. We had to plug our ears when they were firing. The artillerymen had hidden their reserve shells in the hedge at the edge of the path. One day, when we were passing by, fearful as usual, a plane dropped one enormous bomb. We lay down in the grass, expecting the worst. Wouldn't that set off the munitions depot? Then we realized that this thing was not headed for earth in normal fashion, but was drifting slowly down. To our great relief, it landed without exploding; it was only a reservoir of fuel, released by a plane. Of course, we hadn't known that such a thing existed.

During the whole Occupation, we had made it a point of honor not to talk to the Germans; now, the dangers that we had in common brought us together, and we exchanged words. They weren't all tough and mean, especially the older ones. Some showed their family photos. "War is horrible," they confided to us, and they were sincere. Without admitting it, some began to realize that the situation was not in their favor. Under bombings and machine-gun fire, they

---

[21] Here, an old-fashioned wind-up wall clock, marked in Roman numerals.

seemed more fearful than we; of course, they had more experience with the dangers, and knew what they faced as soldiers.

From the time of the Landing, they had lost mastery of the air space. For them, all planes were enemies, and they had to hide from them. In the park of Villeray, in the middle of a flowerbed, there was a lovely 18th century statue of a cherub looking up in the air. An officer with a sense of humor had put a whistle in its mouth and hung a sign around its neck, saying « *Luftsperre* ». The statue had become the watchful guardian angel of the soldiers of the Grand Reich.

At la Bagotière, an officer had use of an amphibious Volkswagen equipped with a radio. One day, when he was looking for a station, I just had time to hear: "The *tricolore*[22] flies over the ruins of Caen." So our city was now freed, but destroyed.[23]

Quick to interpret the least signs, we really felt that the enemy was losing ground. Now, in the lull of the heavy cannoning, the wind sometimes carried the sound of the machine guns.

A calculating farmer lady was able to supplement her farm animals when the soldiers were pushing a large herd before them; she opened the gate just at the right moment, and captured a good number.

And the time came when the soldiers would amuse themselves, shooting and trying to chase me in the fields. I forced myself not to run, to hide my fear; then I found that they were firing blanks.

Bombs had destroyed their battery of huge, deafening 220 mm cannons with no more noise than one of their salutes. Now, they were evacuating. On the vehicle at the head of the convoy, the real *Luftsperre*, whistle between his

---

[22] The three-colored (blue, white and red) flag adopted after the French Revolution.

[23] In fact, 75 per cent of the city of Caen had been destroyed, but most, including meticulously reconstructed stained glass church windows, was later rebuilt.

teeth, was poised to give the alert, as he searched the sky for the bombardiers of the R.A.F. (Royal Air Force). Arriving in pursuit, they loomed into view before long.

Our days were unbelievable, divided between fear and misery. Property was a useless idea, since we lived for no more than one essential goal: not to die!

That particular morning, the troop had not returned, and la Bagotière was strangely empty. A *Feld-Webel* [sergeant] ordered us to remove some items left behind; there was still a washbasin in back, covered with cigars.

I don't know why, but I played the farm boy and wanted one. The task finished, the soldier began to count his cigars. He was missing three: « *Drei Zigaretten !* » ["Three cigars!"] He frisked the valet, who had been careful to leave his jacket at the farm with his booty, while I secretly disposed of mine in the half-light of the barn. We had foolishly fallen for their pre-meditated temptation, allowing them to abuse us verbally and with their boots: "Little French swindler!"

It became obvious that we would be leaving before long. We began to finish off our bottles of hard cider and old Calvados, drinking both at every meal. After an alcoholic lunch, I smoked a retrieved cigar. It made me sick, justifying the proverb, "Ill-gotten goods seldom prosper."

Monsieur Jacques Le Roy Ladurie, whom everyone called « *M'sieur Jacques* », was a captain in the underground Resistance. He arrived unexpectedly, to order the evacuation of the town where he was Mayor. I can still see his head emerging from the secret vault of the château, where we were helping him hide his most beautiful books, the dishes and the silverware. His face, illuminated from below by the light of a candle, looked mysterious to me. In fact, weren't the Germans looking for him?

Then he led me to his wardrobe and offered me the choice of three ties, any that I would like—but only three—so that we wouldn't be unnecessarily loaded down. He spread out an armful on the bed, two or three hundred perhaps. There were ties of all colors—those that he had worn when he was Minister of Agriculture, others that he must have worn only once. I was flabbergasted to be faced with such a choice, astounded that one man could buy himself so many ties.

Early in the morning on the 25th of July, our carts loaded, we evacuated with the whole village, about fifty kilometers out, to the Château du Jardin in Giel, property of Count Dauger, father of Madame Le Roy Ladurie. M'sieur Jacques couldn't bear to leave the Gobelins tapestry behind, so he used it as a beautiful tarpaulin.

In Tournebu, a plane hit by the D.C.A. [French anti-aircraft] fell in flames not far from us. Then we crossed the still-smoking ruins of Falaise. Out of all the rubble, I remember especially a radio set that had been hidden behind the metal curtain of a fireplace, now enthroned in plain view, atop a heap of ruins.

Château du Jardin de Giel (13th century). During the last major bombardments of the Landing, the refugees hid on the (center) tower's dungeon staircase.

At the Château du Jardin de Giel, the war had not yet arrived. We poor refugees, with our dusty load, brought its first indecent picture. Here, the birds were singing and you could not hear the rumbling of battle. The reception was rather cool, but we couldn't blame them: there was no food for extra guests. We asked to be put up where we would be the least trouble.

It was there that I agreed to grind the substitute for coffee and make grilled barley for the German field kitchen cook. To thank me, he generously offered a moldy loaf of brown bread. But at night, how good it was to eat a little when hunger kept me awake.

Our family received some special treatment: instead of bedding with the others in the straw of a barn, we were lodged in the unused roof spaces in the castle, where the genealogical tree of Monsieur le Comte was located—for some reason, on the reverse side of funeral announcements pinned up in the spaces.

Although we had avoided the lack of privacy of the barn, where villagers were thrown together, we did share their meals at a potluck table. Cider was served from a bucket by Léon, a grimy dwarf who plunged in his brown, snuff-taking hand with the quarter-liter goblet that he used to fill our glasses.

The idea of war, with its bombs and shells, soon caught up with the premises' inhabitants, and marvelously improved the consideration of our hosts. Wouldn't they themselves soon be refugees? A pilot came by, machine-gunning so low that we could see his head at the controls. Cartridges rained everywhere, goading the enormous bull in the middle of the lawn, and making him quite furious.

The next day, while I was admiring the wheeling of the "Lightings," those double fuselage fighter-bombers, I realized that I was in the axis of the heavy machine gun shooting at it. That's how a 20 mm shell planted itself in the soil at my feet—without exploding. Which would have deprived you of this story.

I can still feel the cold of the sleepless night of the last attack, when we all thought we would die under the shells from the tanks. We were on the steps in the old stone dungeon, with its enormous walls. This lasted the entire night, and there was no calm until sun-up.

Later, in front of the stable at the farm, four men were firmly holding a splendid racehorse, while the veterinarian tried to pull out shrapnel. Since the flow of blood on his hide was making me nauseous, I set off for a walk, heading to the edge of the park. A German guard sprang from the ditch, taking aim at me: « *Wer da ?* » ["Who's there?"] I raised my arms and returned peacefully to witness the end of the horse's operation.

The hedge of the *Terres Noires* [Black Lands] was burning, ignited by the shellfire. From the main road, beyond the trees, came the uninterrupted noise of a convoy. Later we learned that they were cordoning off the sector of Falaise. Would we really be liberated?

A reconnaissance jeep arrived in the château courtyard, with men dressed in other uniforms and other helmets, and weapons in their hands. They seemed in a hurry, nervous. We stared at them, not believing that this moment, so fervently hoped for these four years, had arrived. They were looking for other Russian soldiers of the *Wehrmacht* [Armed Forces] in their hideout. Proudly we accompanied the voluntary prisoners, who joyfully give us their last cigarettes of powdered tobacco. But the Allies welcomed them roughly, frisking them at gunpoint, as though they were enemies just the same. They loaded them into trucks and, with heavy hearts, we saw them leave, feeling as though we had betrayed friends. The extermination to which they were delivered on returning to the USSR confirmed our premonitions.

Later, we ventured as far as the route to Argentan; the Allied tanks and the curtained cars advanced slowly in a continuous wave. The vehicles were so close together that it was impossible to cross the road. This convoy, whose beginning we had not seen, seemed endless. How had they been able to disembark with all that equipment?

The torsos of the leaders of the tanks emerged from open turrets; they seemed very serious, with their radio sets on their ears, until the moment when we noticed that they were listening to music.

Suddenly, this unimaginable parade, the beginning of which we hadn't seen and the end of which we couldn't know, stopped. Over there, beyond the hills, had they met with resistance? No, they did not go into defense mode, did not re-buckle their war helmets. They came down from their vehicles to settle at the roadside with stoves and mess kits. They were British and we were at the sacred tea time!

These brave soldiers wanted to eat, like everybody. They shared food with us, slices of bread of an unfamiliar whiteness. They offered chocolate, chewing gum and packets of "blond" cigarettes that left a lingering odor on their uniforms. They even had a condom with every ration.

In the ditch, a dead German soldier was in full decomposition, swollen and black. In the eyes of the peasants, he symbolized the enemy; they spat on him, while marveling that a "black man" could be in the German army. The next day, the orphanage in Giel celebrated a dignified burial Mass for him.

We had just one mission: to return home and gather up whatever of our heritage the war had left us. As soon as it was possible, we took the road of the liberated territory, to discover a new world where everything was surprising. We no longer feared being attacked, but everywhere there was this mixed odor of fire, powder and rot.

Dead soldiers were still lying out in the fields, their guns in their hands. Had they been killed by land mines? Arms and munitions from the two camps were strewn everywhere. In a ditch, a whole crate of Panzerfaust [German anti-tank weapons] was fraternizing with scattered English rockets. Dead horses and cows, swollen like toy balloons and covered with flies, poisoned the air with their stench.

The bomb disposal experts had unwound their red and white bands, delimiting their action zone as "Off Bound!"

Behind their Ariane's[24] string, in the fields now without animals, the grass had grown very long. Who would dare risk it?

Trees blown leafless had taken on winter silhouettes. Elsewhere, shells had marked their passage in the foliage with perfectly round holes framing clouds like aspirin tablets.

We learned to recognize other arms, other uniforms, other trucks. The engineers maneuvered machines never before seen. We discovered the first Bulldozer. Bridges that could be taken apart by the engineers were slowly replacing the destroyed stone bridges.

We saluted the convoys we met, and used two fingers to form the Churchill V for Victory, suppressing the thought that this could also be V for Victim. On the rear of the vehicles we translated, without understanding its importance, the reminder painted there: "Keep Right!"[25]

Now, some British soldiers occupied the château of Villeray, which had fortunately been spared. They seemed at ease there, and agreed coldly to let us sleep in a barn. Who could prove to them that these nomads, accompanied by their followers, were the rightful owners? Couldn't we be former collaborators or German spies?

The next day, we continued the return route towards Caen, discovering the virtues of hitchhiking. Mom fainted when she saw that our home was roofless. We were taken in by more fortunate neighbors, whose house was intact.

Near the old washhouse, we could cross the Orne on a pontoon bridge. It dipped each time a car went over it, threatening to throw us into the water. In the midst of the ruins, new rail tracks were born. Some wall sections brought memories of entire streets with their little shops, of which

---

[24] Ariane is Ariadne in Greek mythology. She left a string, threaded through the Labyrinth, to help Theseus find his way out, after he had accomplished his mission of killing the Minotaur on the isle of Crete.

[25] The British, who drive on the left side of the road, needed to keep right, so as not to collide head-on with the French and the Americans.

practically nothing remained. The homes that were left astonished our memories. Even distances seemed changed. It would take months to substitute these new images for those that we remembered.

At home, only the high section of the roof had been destroyed. We salvaged enough tiles to repair the lower part and use two rooms: one for living, the other for salvageable items.

After each downpour, we would go to the second story, sweep the water as you would from the bridge of a ship, and make it run through the holes of shells, into basins placed on the ground floor. After the storm, a strange odor floated down *rue Branville*: a mixture of fresh tar, wet ivy and the pleasing (to me!) scent of Players Navy Cut [a brand of English "blond" cigarettes].

That day, on the Cours Sadi-Carnot, the British gun crew of a D.C.A. joyfully brandished a sign made from a broken door, where they had written with a piece of plaster debris:
"PARIS IS DELIVERED"

It was the 25th of August, 1944.

CHAPTER V MY OWN UNITED STATES OF AMERICA

In "Madeleine," that famous song by Jacques Brel, Madeleine's trembling lover, ever-patient but waiting in vain, sings, "She's America to me."

When I was young, my concept of America was like that—out of reach, attainable only in my dreams. Only much later did I discover "my own United States of America"—not found in any guidebook, written only in my memory and in my heart.

Armand Idrac

Before the war, our parents had driven us one day to Le Havre to see the *Normandie*, that extraordinary ocean liner that could cross the Atlantic in five or six days. I can picture myself, very small, at the end of the dock, looking up and down its wall of window-pierced steel plates. That wall was as insurmountable for me as the ocean that the great ship crossed so easily.

In those days, we encountered very few Americans, and they were striking in their different styles of dress: the Texans kept their ten-gallon hats on their heads, and the older women continued to dress in the vivid colors of their youth. We admired their outward signs of wealth and assumed that, since they could make such a trip, they were rich, and represented all Americans.

Later, at the time of the Liberation, we encountered many more Americans—soldiers who ate white bread, chewed gum, gave out chocolate and also smoked Gauloise Blondes cigarettes. They restored our broken-up roads with powerful, new machines that we could only call by their own names for them, such as *bulldozer* and "*cater-pillar*." With those wonderful Belley engineering bridges and their pieces assembled like parts of a giant robot, they replaced the destroyed works of art. Hitchhiking had become a normal means of getting from one place to another. The soldiers willingly took us aboard jeeps, trucks, and even enormous amphibian vehicles.

I will never forget my first visit to the American Military Cemetery at Saint-Laurent-sur-Mer. Planners were still laying it out, and from the mound of earth piled up for the main monument, I saw thousands of wooden crosses aligned and extending endlessly to the sea. There, we could still see wreckage from the ships that would never take them back to their country.

I've returned regularly to this place of remembrance, but never have I been as deeply moved before so many graves. In this now very beautiful setting overlooking the sea, the landscape has given up its cruelty, for, in spite of the wind-borne sea spray, the French have cultivated trees there that stay green all year. The trees reach as far as the cye can see, across the immense field of resting places. The poor wooden crosses have all been replaced with crosses or stars of David fashioned in Carrara marble—a beautiful white veined with green. They are aligned perfectly in every direction.[26]

Around the superb center monument, symbol of resurrection raised to the glory of the fallen soldiers, the names of those that could not be found are engraved on the wall. On the tombs of unidentified remains, one reads the simple inscription "UNKNOWN," throughout entire squared-off areas. On other tombs, the engraved name is inscribed with two dates, the rank, the regiment and the state of origin. Only Franklin D. Roosevelt's son is modestly set apart, with a gilded inscription.

At the other extremity of the terrain stands a round temple of elegant simplicity, open to all beliefs. Although there are many visitors, it is a place of silence and meditation.

The pole bearing the American flag is reflected in the water lily pond. Morning and evening, the colors are raised

---

[26] Approximately nine thousand American soldiers are buried in the American Military Cemetery above Omaha Beach.

and lowered to the strains of the national hymn, played by an invisible, ghostlike orchestra, whose sounds flood the site. It is then that the American visitors are set apart: they stand still, right hand placed over the heart for the duration of "The Star-Spangled Banner."

Very moved, I think of all the young men come from so far for an ideal of liberty—dying on our land, a place unknown to them. They are from Pennsylvania, Iowa, Idaho, New Mexico, Texas, Colorado, Florida, and other states. As I read these names, images of states that I have come to know parade through my head—from the sumptuous, calm forests of Maine, to the majestic Rockies, to the splendid settings of the Far West. How could they leave the wonder of all that?

Quelle connerie la guerre ! [What damned stupidity war is!!]

Some years after the War, I learned of The Experiment in International Living. This American association was created by veterans to foster friendships among young people of all countries, in the belief that a better knowledge of others will help prevent wars. During the years that we received these American students *en demi-pension* [lodging and two meals per day] in our home, they followed courses for two months at the University of Caen, and on weekends we took them on outings in the region.

Living with our friendly family, they considered us their adoptive French parents, and there were wonderful conversations with our children, who saw very soon the usefulness of knowing foreign languages.

I couldn't possibly write of the score or so of guests that we hosted, cared for, loved. Actually, very few have continued to keep in touch! But realistically, we would have had trouble following a correspondence with each of them. Some have come back with their parents, their spouse, their pupils. We have even been able to respond to invitations to visit, when we traveled to the U.S.A.

Long ago, when I began to work at the SNCF [French railroad], I could see the trains passing by my office, which was next to rail lines from Paris to Cherbourg. At that time, the "Queens"[27] stopped over regularly at Cherbourg, between sailings from Southampton, England to New York. Normally, there were three trains for each transatlantic crossing. All this gave me something to daydream about. I wanted to go to the U.S., but the trip by sea was too expensive and too slow for me. And there was the risk of getting seasick.

Then, with the beginning of charter flights and the 747s, it all became possible!

Yes, America was far, and it was big. For a long time, I tried to devise a trip as complete as possible, to discover this country that we dreamed about. But the solution was simple: several trips had to be planned. And that is what we did.

On that first trip, we arrived in Boston. Mary, one of our former student guests, met us there for an overnight stay at the townhouse of some friends who had left her the key. What a pleasure, how happy we were to see Mary again, after so many years!

Here are some of the places that we went on to visit during our many trips to the United States:

Denver, Colorado;
The "Wild West," where we saw Native Americans;
Flamingo, the Florida Everglades, and the "10,000 Islands" near Naples, Florida;
Sacramento, California and a restored "ghost town";
Death Valley with the lowest spot (282 feet below sea level) in the Western Hemisphere;
Lake Badwater, so salty that it never dries up, even in temperatures recorded in excess of 134° F;
Palo Alto and the beautiful San Francisco Bay area;
Hollywood and the Napa Valley, California;
Philadelphia, its outlying Amish country and Valley Forge, Pennsylvania.

---

[27] The British cruise ships Queen Mary and Queen Elizabeth.

In Philadelphia, of course, the first historic site to visit is Independence Mall and the Liberty Bell, struck by Benjamin Franklin himself in 1777 to mark the independence of the United States. As a symbol of freedom, the bell was also rung when the slaves were emancipated and upon the Landing in Normandy in 1944, to announce the beginning of the Liberation of France. The Liberty Bell means a great deal to our American friends, and plans are underway to place a copy in the American Cemetery of Saint-Laurent-sur-Mer.

Abbaye aux Dames CAEN

Normandy Liberty Bell

Pictured above, the Normandy Liberty Bell is an exact replica of the United States' Liberty Bell, and is tuned to the same E-flat note that once sounded before the Liberty Bell cracked in 1846. Patrick Daudon, a former mayor in Normandy, commissioned this replica to coincide with the 60th anniversary of the D-Day Allied invasion. He chose the Liberty Bell because it had been struck seven times on D-Day by the Philadelphia mayor to spell out the word "Liberty."

The Normandy Liberty Bell was first rung on June 6, 2004 on the shores of Normandy to commemorate the 60th anniversary of D-Day, and was first rung in the United States on July 4, 2005 outside of Liberty Bell Center on Independence Mall as part of the "Let Freedom Ring" ceremony. Starting in July 2005 at Philadelphia's Constitution Center, the Normandy Liberty Bell will tour the United States for a period of two years.

There is so much more that I could write about the awe-inspiring United States, but I'll finish with some final impressions.

On one trip, we stood at the Canadian border marveling at the famous Niagara Falls, one of the most impressive sights in the world.

The natural parks of the West, one more beautiful than another, must be mentioned, although I don't intend to compete with the Michelin guides. Here are just a few of my unforgettable memories of their beauty:

- The indescribable marvel of the Grand Canyon, with Colorado split into a furrow 1600 meters deep;
- Monument Valley, in the upper course of the Rio Grande, with its striking rock formation, the natural background of so many films;
- Salt Lake City, the "Mecca" of the Mormons, its gigantic copper quarry open to the sky;
- Mount Rushmore sculpted into colossal heads representing those four famous presidents of the United States: George Washington, Thomas Jefferson, Theodore Roosevelt and Abraham Lincoln.

A "special mention" award goes to Yellowstone National Park in Wyoming, at an altitude of 2400 meters. This was the first established National Park. It is as big as France's island of Corsica. Yellowstone has more than 200 geysers, including the celebrated "Old Faithful"; all sorts of volcanic evidence; lakes of different colors; immense agglomerates of snow-white chalk; canyons; abundant waterfalls 150 meters high and audible kilometers away. While hiking there, we chanced on various animals—bison, deer, brown bears, and grizzlies.

If today, health reasons prevent me from enjoying the USA, I have come full circle, for America has once again become, as in my youth, an inaccessible dream. But now I have these unforgettable memories of a country so close to my heart.

*

* *

Editor's note: Armand Idrac and his family continue to receive American visitors.

In March 2005, Professor Christine Gaudry-Hudson (far left), Head of Foreign Languages at Millersville University in Pennsylvania, together with her French students, dined with Armand and Yvonne Idrac in the festive ambience of a restaurant in Caen. The students had studied from both the French and the English full versions of the Memoirs, and had prepared discussion topics on World War II. Armand, ever the *raconteur,* carried forth with the good humor that pervades his story-telling.

*

* *

On July 15, 2005, Armand and Yvonne Idrac (far right), with their daughter Agnes and her children, welcomed a group of 16 American French teachers who had come to Caen for an immersion program with the group The French Traveler, based in Sarasota, Florida. The director of the program, Valerie Sutter (fourth from left, second row), is a former French teacher and former Secretary-Treasurer of the American Association of Teachers of French, Eastern Massachusetts chapter.

APPENDIX

Editor's note:

Most readers, both young and old, can identify with the broken-hearted sweetness of the youngster in this story. In his youth, Armand wrote short stories and *The Story of the Little Soldier Who Went to War against the Russians* was awarded the Diploma of Honor *Jeux Floraux* of Tunis 1951.

The following short story, *Amo Josiam [Latin: I Love Josée]* shows his most fully developed lyrical expression.

Armand mentions that the bombs were dropping, providing World War II as the history-changing backdrop for a story of teenagers growing into the adult world, as all children inevitably do, despite their circumstances.

AMO JOSIAM

With half shut eyes, I lightly inclined my head, but I couldn't really see her face any more, her little girl's face that was lost during the war. I only remember her eyes, blue eyes like sweet almonds. I no longer recall her child's face, but I still seem to hear her thin voice taking on the inflections of a young woman, to confide to me: "You know, I'll be in *sixième*[28] when school starts up, and I'll learn Latin."

For me, the simple fact that she would learn Latin was a wonder. I imagined her already speaking the strange language of my Mass book, and it seemed that the idea of learning Latin surprised and moved her, as it did me.

I must have been in love with her for a very long time, perhaps since the day when, pressed on the same chaise lounge, we listened as her brother told the story of *Les Aventures du Roi de l'Or*. I couldn't have known her without loving her, and I had known her for such a long time that I must not have existed before knowing her.

Saying « *Bonsoir* », I took pleasure in pressing her little hand very firmly between my two hands, and I held it there for a long time; but she, unlike me, hadn't read bad books, and probably understood nothing by this gesture, which to me seemed an unspeakably bold move—a lover's move.

As a pious Sunday choirboy, I didn't take my eyes off her, and each time that the priest pronounced the word "love," I signaled her with my eyes. My burning cheeks took on the color of my cape. I could see Josée look at me like that sometimes, too.

But her indifference to thousands of little nothings threw me into despair. Day by day, I was more and more intent on making her feel more strongly towards me. Often, I would

---

[28] In the U.S., approximately sixth grade.

dream that she came softly, placing her arm around my neck and pressing her mouth to my ear, whispering words of love that I had waited for, for such a long time. Waking, I would caress the spot on my ear that her lips had chosen.

One day, we were playing in my yard. When it was her brother's turn to wait for us to hide, I told Josée to follow me, I knew a good place. I pulled her behind a grove of spindle trees, and whispered, "I love you, Josée." She screamed "Idiot!" as she did when she stuck herself while sewing for her dolls. Her brother hollered, "Ninety-nine, one hundred" in the distance.

—And you, do you love me?

—Maybe!

Doubtless, she had never been asked the question.

I came out red-faced from the ordeal and, fearing embarrassing questions at home, I passed a wet handkerchief over my face. But I was in such an anxious state that the remedy proved worse than the sickness. It felt as though my cheeks would burst, like over-ripe tomatoes.

The next day, her brother reproached me severely. She had told him everything and this brat—a year younger than I—laid a reprimand on me that started like this: "I kid you not, if it weren't for me, Josée would tell our parents."

I couldn't convince myself not to believe him; I went cold at the very idea of the catastrophe that he claimed to have spared me. Moreover, I had lost all his respect with this one act.

One of my naughty friends, in whom I foolishly confided this misadventure, took a superior air, and declared: "You know, you must be crazy; you have to tell this little girl that you love her, in Latin: « *Amo Josiam !* » He had a way of saying "this little girl" in a scornful, bemused tone that reduced my idol to nothingness. I admired his scorn at the same time as it bothered me deeply.

Sometimes, when we would see Josée in the distance, he would order, in his rough, already-changing voice: "Go on, guy! Go on! Holler to her: « *Amo Josiam !* » I trembled, fearing she would hear. This « *Amo Josiam* » from his mouth seemed like blasphemy. The lout, he couldn't love her like I loved her. « *Amo Josiam !* » he would call out to me in the street. « *Amo Josiam !* » he would holler into the open doors of the echoing corridors. I suffered painfully from his game. « *Amo Josiam* », I caught myself murmuring, like a prayer. « *Amo Josiam* », like a sob without a tear. « *Amo Josiam* », sweet yet cruel.

I happened to see her every day, on the way to school. Loving to eat, she enjoyed my vitamin cakes; being able to please her comforted me enormously.

Then I discovered, in a big red book, the immortal sonnet of Arvers:

> My soul has its secret, my life has its mystery
> An eternal love conceived in one moment...

He translated my feelings so faithfully that it astounded me. I plagiarized him immediately, confident that I wouldn't be found out. We met alone and I gave her the sonnet, saying offhandedly that I had written it for her.

Josée seemed truly moved. She must have found it so beautiful that she let her very best friend read it. The friend came up to us, read through the paper and declared promptly, in a cool, snobbish tone: "That's funny, I've already read that somewhere!" It was some time before I dared to again see Josée or her best friend.

World War II was in progress, and the bombs were going off every night. Josée's parents decided to leave for the countryside until the war was over. The night before she left, I went to say good-bye to my friend. She was alone, gathering flowers in the garden. For an instant I thought that our good-byes would be emotional, and I wanted to keep the memory forever. She reached through the flowers and held my hand and, without looking at me, said a simple « *Au revoir !* » [Good-bye!], as if I were to see her tomorrow. Then she resumed humming, "As the blue bell mounts the hill..."

I turned around, heavy-hearted with all my unappreciated, neglected love. Passing the rose garden, I heard her again, still humming "As the blue bell mounts the hill…"

Pain from disappointing good-byes, scent of roses, songs, I tasted it all on my exodus, to the tune of this miserable German tune that I whistled, "As the blue bell mounts the hill…"

A tune, the smell of roses, the memory of my beloved seen through the flowers—these haunted the sleepless night of the last attack, when we thought that we would surely die under the shells of the tanks. Like a fool, I tried to think of her the whole night, to be sure that my last thoughts would be of her…

Afterwards, waiting hours for the distribution of water from the cistern-truck which never did arrive, I encountered Josée again. She seemed even more beautiful to me in the midst of so much misery, so much horror.

When school resumed, we had classes at the same times, and we had to take almost the same route to school. We saw each other often, and my classmates made jealous, embarrassing remarks. But the pest that I hated the most was Bastuccio, a spindly kid who was at least four classes younger than I. Every time he saw me alone, he would run up, to walk with me. His manners were so refined that I couldn't be rude to him. He never failed to ask courteously for news of « *Mademoiselle ton Amie* » ["Mademoiselle, your friend"].

I would always answer somehow, trying to be modest, but I feel sorry now that I gave the impression that « *Mademoiselle mon Amie* » was rather insignificant to me. But he wasn't fooled, and it seemed to me that he enjoyed making an "older person" take the trouble to try to fool him.

« *Mademoiselle mon Amie* » had shown me a photograph of herself in a romantic pose, and I begged her to give it to me. "You can't be serious!" she said. Then she promised to ask her mother's permission. The next day, warning me not to say anything about it, she gave me her picture.

It was a gift of herself that she gave, and my head was in the clouds. I forgot the time of my class, the snow, the frozen earth. Again, I picture myself entering class late, into the midst of chilled pupils. They began to tap their feet in the freezing room, hollering louder and louder: "Light a fire, some fire!" I didn't feel the cold, but I remember precisely that scene, and I wanted no part of it; I pressed her slender silhouette, in an envelope, against my chest.

A pale winter sun lit up the windows, frosted with softly melting flowers. They called out to me: "So you're not cold, you're not stomping your feet?" No, I wasn't cold, and no one else in my place would have been cold. No, I wasn't cold, the melting ice held all the sorrows of my unhappy Love. But they were melting, and only joy would remain, all the joy of my Love burning in the sun. I started to tap my feet, too, so as not to appear cowardly, but while they were hollering "Light a fire! Some fire!" I thought I heard them all exclaim, with that same verve: "Josée! Josée!"

I hid her picture in the covers of books and in my notebooks, between sheets of folded blotting paper. I couldn't do without her image, as I couldn't do without her. This passion was my happiness, but it also threw me into confusion. It was terribly important to me because it stayed uncertain, fragile, incomplete.

Josée! There were days when you made fun of me, when you cruelly enjoyed describing the lover of your dreams, that shadowy being that you always described as having different features from mine. I was tall, he would have been short. I was brown-haired, he would have been blond. And you were mean and laughed at this cruel game. And your friend laughed, too. It did me no good not to believe in the game; it hurt me terribly, with the sharp pain of a physical illness.

There were also days when you loved me! Days when you let me believe that you would never hurt me again. One Thursday, when I was passing in front of your house, you glued your little pink nose against the windowpane. I could just make out the direction of your gaze, and your nose was pressed so hard against the glass that it appeared as a little white, round spot. I will never forget that little nose glued against the pane, and you, looking at me passing by…

Another day, when we were reading the same book together, I ventured to put my arm around your shoulders. I pressed you softly against me, and I could feel the wildest of your locks tickle my cheek. I had only to turn my head to kiss you. I was sure that you would like that, too. At that moment, your brother came in. Why did I never again put my arm around you?

I put up with your spoiled little girl whims, and ended up all the sadder because you plunged me from pain to joy and back again. Then, when I couldn't take it any more, one day I had to confess all this. Before you ran off, you quickly murmured with those adorable little lips: "Let's be friends, I don't love you!"

I never saw you again. Never again! So you became the magic fairy in my childhood picture book. With time, this shadow self became still more beautiful, incredibly sweet. I had clarified it little by little in my sorrow, from the souvenir of the Josée who had given me so much joy and done so much harm, in order to have from this adorable little girl only the memory of her eyes, with no memory of her face. The memory of a childhood Josée who therefore had never truly existed.

REFERENCES

SELECTED BIBLIOGRAPHY

Asselin, Gilles & Ruth Mastron. *Au Contraire! Figuring Out the French.* Yarmouth, Maine: Intercultural Press, 2001.

Barnett, Barbara P. *Faces of the Holocaust: Marcel Jabelot.* Wayne, PA: Beach Lloyd Publishers, LLC, 2004.

Carell, Paul. *Invasion—they're coming! The German account of the Allied landings and the 80 days' battle for France.* Translated from the German *Sie Kommen!: die Invasion 1944* by E. Osers. New York: Dutton, 1963.

Cretzmeyer, Stacy. *Your Name is Renée: Ruth Kapp Hartz's Story as a Hidden Child in Nazi-Occupied France.* Foreword by Beate Klarsfeld. New York: Oxford University Press, 1999.

D'Este, Carlo. *Decision in Normandy.* New York: E. P. Dutton, Inc., 1983.

Ghiglione, Margaret & Carol Pouchol, eds. Charts. *AAWE Guide to Education.* Paris: AAWE 6th edition, 2003.

Hastings, Max. *Overlord: D-Day and the battle for Normandy.* New York: Simon and Schuster, 1984.

Keegan, John. *The First World War.* New York: A. Knopf, 1999.

Mayle, Peter & Judith Clancy, Illustrator. *A Year in Provence.* Vancouver, WA: Vintage Books; Reprint edition, 1991.

Platt, Polly & Ande Grchich, Illustrator. *Savoir-Flair: 211 Tips for Enjoying France and the French.* Skokie, Ill: Distribooks, 2001.

Ryan, Cornelius. *The Longest Day: The Classic Epic of D-Day.* New York: Touchstone Books, 1994.

Zuccotti, Susan. *The Holocaust, the French and the Jews.* New York: BasicBooks, 1993.

PERIODICALS

"Alexis de Tocqueville." In Depth Review. *News from France.* April 13, 2005.

"Letters Bring D-Day Back to Life." *News from France.* June 11, 2003.

Normandy's Conquering Spirit: The 50th Anniversary of D-Day. Spec. issue of *FRANCE Magazine.* The Maison Française: Washington, D.C. Winter 1993-94.

"Ten Reasons to Study in France." *France Today: Educational Issue.* August 11, 2000.

"Tombs of U.S. Soldiers Honored in France." *News from France.* September 3, 2003.

VIDEOGRAPHY

Au Revoir Les Enfants (Good-bye Children). Dir. by Louis Malle. Perf. Gaspard Manesse, Raphael Fejto. Orion Pictures Corporation, 1987.

Faces of the Holocaust. (Marcel Jabelot) French with English Subtitles. Exec. Producer, Barbara Barnett. Producers, Martha Goell Lubell & Sharon Mullally.
Dir. of Photography Toni A. Banet. 1995.

The Longest Day. Dir. Ken Annakin, Andrew Marton, Bernhard Wicki, Darryl F. Zanuck. Perf. John Wayne, Robert Mitchum, Henry Fonda, Richard Burton. 20th Century Fox, 1962.

Saving Private Ryan. Dir. Steven Spielberg. Perf. Tom Hanks, Edward Burns, Tom Sizemore, Matt Damon. Written by Robert Rodat. DreamWorks Pictures and Paramount Pictures, 1998.

WEBOGRAPHY (2003–2005)

[Alexis De Tocqueville.] Brainy Quote. <http://www.brainyquote.com/quotes/authors/a/alexis_detoqueville.htm>

[Alexis de Tocqueville.] Special Introduction to Book One of *Democracy in America* by Hon. John T. Morgan. <http://authorsdirectory.com/b/1dinaio.htm>

American Association of Teachers of French. <http://www.frenchteachers.org>

Death-Valley.US Climate. <http://www.death-valley.us/climate.html>

Les Etats-Unis de A à Z. Outline of French Educational System. <http://www.amb-usa.fr/irc/faq/scsystem.htm>

FrancePress, Inc. <http://www.journalfrancais.com> <http://www.francetoday.com>

French Embassy Press and Information Service. <http://www.ambafrance-us.org> <http://www.france.diplomatie.gouv.fr>

The French Tutorial. frenchtutorial.com, Hervé Foucher, 1999–2002. <http://www.helio.org/education/french/vocabulary/ learning_system.html>

The Landing Beaches. <http://www.150th.com/letters/omahabch.htm>

News from France: A triweekly review of French news and trends. Online at <http://www.ambafrance-us.org/publi/nff>

[untitled]. <http://www.normandy-tourism.org/w/pdf/GTPlanner.pdf>

World War II Online. Playnet Inc. <http://www.hq.wwiionline.com/journal/war_story_5.shtml>

SUGGESTED DISCUSSION TOPICS

1. (Foreword) Comment on the journal of Marie Le Roy Ladurie. Have you ever kept a diary during a stressful or important event? What might you "read between the lines" of her journal?

2. In general, how would you describe the tone and vocabulary of Armand's memoirs?

3. This book is a translation from the French. If you have read the original French version, do you have comments on the translation?

4. (page 5) Armand is pictured at the age of five, at the steps of the family home in Caen. His present home is just yards away. Do you know anyone in this country or elsewhere who still lives in or near his/her childhood home?

5. (pages 5-10) (a) Do you know of a town like Douvres that has changed considerably since you first visited it? Discuss the changes and whether you welcome them or not.
(b) If you do not know an area that has undergone great change, interview a parent or grandparent who remembers such a transformation, and discuss it with the group.

6. (pages 14-17) "Alcide" was greatly admired, and unforgettable. If you have had such a teacher or mentor, what traits did you admire the most, and how did that person affect you?

7. (page 19) Notice that in the Grade Equivalencies chart, 5 points out of 20 is considered passing. How does that compare with the grading system in your schools?

8. (page 28) What do you know about the Occupied and the "Free" zones in France during World War II? Research this topic.

9. In France and in other European countries, members of the Resistance and Jews were arrested and deported by the Nazis. What other groups were also persecuted? Use the Reference section and other resources to research this topic.

10. (pages 55-57) Have you ever hosted a foreign exchange student? If so, what do you consider necessary for a successful homestay in another country?

11. Have you ever been an exchange student or an exchange teacher? Have you ever engaged in a foreign language "immersion" program? If so, what were your goals, and did you meet those goals? Discuss the total experience.

12. Prepare a report on Alexis de Tocqueville, including the following:
Basic biographical information;
The political and social scene of his era;
Highlights of his best-known work, *Democracy in America.*

13. It has been said that France and the United States are like siblings—perhaps sisters—alternating over time between a warm relationship and a difficult one. Comment on this observation.

14. Living through World War II as a young teenager no doubt affected Armand in many ways. What more recent life-changing events closer to home come to mind?

15. If you have met any veterans of World War II, discuss whatever they may have shared with you of their war experiences.

Beach Lloyd
PUBLISHERS
LLC

Web: http://www.BEACHLLOYD.com
E-mail: BEACHLLOYD@erols.com
Phone: (610) 407-0130 or
Toll-free: 1-866-218-3253, Ext. 8668
Fax: (775) 254-0633

P.O.Box 2183
Southeastern, PA 19399-2183

QUICK Order Form

🖷 **Fax orders**: 775-254-0633. Send this form.

☎ **Telephone orders**: Call 610-407-0130 or toll free 1-866-218-3253, Ext. 8668.

💻 **E-mail orders**: BEACHLLOYD@erols.com

🖃 **Postal Orders**: Beach Lloyd Publishers, LLC
Joanne S. Silver, Mgr.
P.O. Box 2183
Southeastern PA 19399-2183
USA

Please send the following books & other products:

____

____

____

Name: __________________________________

Address: ________________________________

City: ______________ State: _____ ZIP: _______

Telephone: ____________________

E-mail address: ________________

Sales tax: Please add 6% for products shipped to Pennsylvania addresses.
Shipping: **U.S.**: $2-4
International: $5-9, contact for estimate.
Payment: Check or Money Order in US dollars, payable to Beach Lloyd Publishers, LLC.
Visit www.BEACHLLOYD.com for products and pricing.